THE LYON TRAVELER'S GUIDE 2023

An Insider's Guide to the Best of France's Second City. Uncovering the City's Culture, Cuisine and History

By

Leonard Shriner

Contents

INTRODUCTION

Lyon is a city that has long captured the hearts of travellers from around the world. Nestled in the heart of France's Rhône-Alpes region, it is a city that is renowned for its rich history, beautiful architecture, and mouth-watering cuisine. From its cobbled streets and winding alleyways to its world-class museums and lively cultural scene, Lyon has something for everyone.

Lyon is one of the oldest cities in France, dating back to Roman times. It was founded in 43 BC as a military outpost on the banks of the Rhône and Saône rivers. Over the centuries, Lyon grew in importance and became a center for trade, silk weaving, and printing. Today, Lyon is known as the gastronomic capital of France, thanks to its many Michelin-starred restaurants, bustling food markets, and traditional bouchons.

One of the most striking features of Lyon is its architecture. The city is home to a wealth of historic buildings, including Gothic cathedrals, Renaissance palaces, and art nouveau masterpieces. The UNESCO World Heritage site of Vieux Lyon is particularly notable, with its beautiful old buildings and narrow streets. Visitors can also explore Lyon's many museums, which cover everything from art and history to science and technology.

Lyon is also a city of culture. It has a thriving music scene, with concerts and festivals taking place throughout the year. The city is home to the National Orchestra of Lyon, as well as several other ensembles and performance spaces. Lyon's theater scene is equally impressive, with productions ranging from classical plays to contemporary works. The city also hosts a number of film festivals, including the famous Lumière Festival, which celebrates the work of the Lumière brothers, who invented the motion picture camera.

Of course, no discussion of Lyon would be complete without mentioning its cuisine. Lyon is a paradise for food lovers, with its many markets, food shops, and restaurants. The city is particularly known for its bouchons, which are small, traditional restaurants that serve hearty, homestyle dishes. These establishments have a unique atmosphere, with red-and-white checkered tablecloths, carafes of wine, and convivial conversation. Visitors to Lyon can also sample the city's many cheeses, including Saint-Marcellin and Roquefort, as well as its famous saucisson (sausage).

Lyon's culinary reputation extends beyond its traditional dishes, however. The city has a number of Michelin-starred restaurants, including Paul Bocuse, which is widely regarded as one of the best restaurants in the world. Visitors can also explore Lyon's many wine bars, which offer a wide range of local wines, including Beaujolais and Côtes du Rhône. In fact, Lyon is home to the Cité du Vin, a museum and cultural center dedicated to the history and culture of wine.

But Lyon is not just a city for foodies and culture vultures. It is also a city that is easy to explore on foot or by bike. Lyon's extensive network of bike paths and pedestrian zones make it a pleasure to explore on two wheels or on foot. Visitors can stroll along the banks of the Rhône and Saône rivers or climb up to Fourvière Hill for panoramic views of the city. Lyon is also home to several parks and gardens, including the Parc de la Tête d'Or, which is one of the largest urban parks in Europe.

In conclusion, Lyon is a city that has something for everyone. Whether you're interested in history, culture, food, or just enjoying the outdoors, Lyon is a city that will captivate you. Its rich heritage and lively cultural scene make it one of the most dynamic and exciting cities in

France, while its gastronomy scene has earned it a well-deserved reputation as a food lover's paradise. Whether you're looking to explore the city's historic landmarks, sample its delicious cuisine, or simply soak up its vibrant atmosphere, Lyon is a destination that is sure to delight.

Lyon is also a city that is constantly evolving, with new restaurants, bars, and cultural spaces opening all the time. This makes it an exciting destination for travelers who are looking for something fresh and new. Whether you're interested in exploring Lyon's cutting-edge art scene, discovering its latest culinary trends, or simply enjoying the city's laid-back lifestyle, Lyon is a city that is always full of surprises.

Finally, Lyon is a city that is easy to get to, with excellent transport links to the rest of France and Europe. The city is served by two airports, as well as several train stations, making it a convenient destination for travelers from around the world. And once you arrive in Lyon, you'll find that the city is easy to navigate, with a well-connected public transport system and plenty of pedestrian zones and bike paths.

In summary, Lyon is a city that has it all. With its rich history, beautiful architecture, and vibrant cultural scene, it is a destination that is sure to capture your heart. And with its mouth-watering cuisine, friendly locals, and relaxed lifestyle, it is a city that you will never want to leave. Whether you're planning a short break or a longer stay, Lyon is a destination that is not to be missed.

CHAPTER 1: LYON'S HISTORY: FROM THE ROMAN EMPIRE TO MODERN TIMES

Lyon is a city with a rich and fascinating history that stretches back more than 2,000 years. It was established by the Romans in 43 BC and immediately became a significant hub for trade and business. Throughout the ages, it has significantly influenced the political, cultural, and economic environment of France and Europe.

The Roman period is one of the most important and influential eras in Lyon's history. The city was founded by the Roman general Munatius Plancus as a strategic military outpost on the banks of the Rhône and Saône rivers. It was soon transformed into a thriving commercial center, with merchants from all over the Roman Empire coming to Lyon to trade in goods such as textiles, pottery, and wine. The city was also home to a thriving community of craftsmen who produced everything from bronze statues to mosaics.

One of the most impressive Roman legacies in Lyon is the Amphitheater of the Three Gauls. This vast arena, which could seat up to 20,000 spectators, was used for gladiatorial contests and other public spectacles. Today, it is one of the best-preserved examples of a Roman amphitheater in France.

During the Middle Ages, Lyon continued to prosper as a center for trade and commerce. The city was a major hub for the silk trade, with merchants from Italy, Spain, and other parts of Europe coming to Lyon to purchase the famous "Lyonnais silk". The city's importance as a center for silk production led to the development of a thriving banking industry, and Lyon became one of the wealthiest cities in Europe.

The Renaissance was another important era in Lyon's history. The city's architectural heritage is particularly rich from this period, with many fine examples of Gothic and Renaissance buildings still standing today. One of the most impressive examples is the Basilica of Notre Dame de Fourvière, which was built in the late 19th century to commemorate the end of the Franco-Prussian War. Its ornate façade, with its colorful mosaics and elaborate sculptures, is a masterpiece of neo-Byzantine architecture.

The 18th century was a time of great change and transformation for Lyon. The city underwent a major urban renewal program, with many of its medieval buildings and narrow streets being replaced by wide boulevards and neoclassical buildings. The city also played a key role in the French Revolution, with many of its citizens actively involved in the events that led to the downfall of the monarchy. Lyon was briefly the capital of France during this period, and it was during this time that the city's famous Place des Terreaux was created.

Lyon saw enormous wealth throughout the 19th century as the city rose to prominence as a hub for manufacturing and industry. Textiles, chemicals, and machinery were among the many products that were produced in Lyon during this period, and the city's population grew rapidly as a result. The city also became an important center for the arts, with many famous writers, painters, and musicians making their homes in Lyon.

During World War II, Lyon played an important role in the French Resistance. The city was a hub for underground resistance networks, and many of its citizens risked their lives to help Allied soldiers and Jewish refugees escape from Nazi persecution. The city's Resistance Museum, located in the former Gestapo headquarters, pays tribute to the bravery and sacrifice of those who fought for freedom during this dark period in history.

In the postwar period, Lyon continued to grow and prosper, with many new industries and businesses setting up shops in the city. The city also became a major center for research and innovation, with many scientific institutes and universities being established in Lyon during this period.

Today, Lyon is a vibrant and modern city that has successfully preserved its rich cultural and architectural heritage while embracing the latest trends and technologies. Visitors to Lyon can explore the city's fascinating history through its many museums, galleries, and monuments while also enjoying its modern amenities and attractions.

One of the best ways to explore Lyon's history is through its many historic landmarks and buildings. The Old Town, or Vieux Lyon, is a UNESCO World Heritage Site and is home to many of the city's most important historic buildings and monuments. Highlights include the stunning Gothic Cathedral of St. John, the ancient Roman theater, and the impressive Renaissance-era Hôtel de Ville, or city hall.

Another must-see attraction is the Musée Gallo-Romain de Lyon, which houses an extensive collection of Roman artifacts and offers a fascinating insight into Lyon's ancient past. The Musée des Beaux-Arts de Lyon is also worth a visit, with its impressive collection of paintings, sculptures, and decorative arts from the Renaissance to the present day.

Food lovers should not miss the opportunity to sample Lyon's famous cuisine, which is renowned throughout France and beyond. The city's traditional bouchons, or small bistros, offer hearty and delicious meals that are based on local ingredients and traditions. Some of the most popular dishes include sausages, tripe, and roast pork, as well as local cheeses and wines.

In addition to its culinary delights, Lyon is also a center for the arts and culture. The city is home to a vibrant arts scene, with many theaters, music venues, and galleries showcasing the latest in contemporary art and performance. Lyon also hosts a number of major cultural events throughout the year, including the famous Fête des Lumières, or Festival of Lights, which attracts millions of visitors each year.

Lyon's transportation infrastructure is also a testament to its modernity and efficiency. The city boasts an extensive public transport network, including buses, trams, and metro lines, which makes it easy to navigate and explore. Lyon is also home to two major train stations, as well as an international airport, which provides easy access to destinations throughout Europe and beyond.

In conclusion, Lyon's history is a rich and fascinating tapestry of the Roman conquest, medieval commerce, Renaissance art and architecture, and modern industry and innovation. Visitors to Lyon can explore this history through its many landmarks, museums, and cultural events while also enjoying its famous cuisine, vibrant arts scene, and modern amenities. Lyon is definitely a city for all seasons and all tourists with its flawless fusion of heritage and contemporary.

CHAPTER 2: LYON'S ARCHITECTURE: FROM GOTHIC CATHEDRALS TO RENAISSANCE PALACES

Lyon is renowned for its architecture, which reflects the city's long and fascinating history. From its Gothic cathedrals to its Renaissance palaces, Lyon's architectural heritage is a testament to the city's rich cultural and artistic traditions.

One of Lyon's most iconic landmarks is the Gothic Cathedral of St. John, which dates back to the 12th century. Located in the heart of the city's Old Town, the cathedral is known for its stunning stained glass windows, intricate carvings, and towering spires. Visitors can explore the cathedral's interior, which is filled with treasures such as a 14th-century astronomical clock and a collection of ornate choir stalls.

Another must-see architectural gem is the Basilica of Notre Dame de Fourvière, which sits atop a hill overlooking the city. Built-in the late 19th century, the basilica is an impressive example of Neo-Byzantine architecture and is adorned with intricate mosaics, frescoes, and stained glass windows. Visitors can climb the basilica's tower for panoramic views of the city and the surrounding countryside.

Lyon's Renaissance architecture is also a major draw for visitors. One of the most impressive examples is the Hôtel de Ville, or city hall, which was built in the 17th century. The building features a stunning façade decorated with sculptures and ornate carvings, as well as a grand staircase and opulent reception rooms.

Another Renaissance-era masterpiece is the Palais de la Bourse, which was built in the mid-19th century as a chamber of commerce. The building features a striking façade adorned with statues of famous merchants and is home to the Musée des Tissus, a museum dedicated to textiles and fabrics.

Lyon's architectural heritage is not limited to its historic buildings and landmarks. The city is also known for its modern architecture, with many innovative and eye-catching structures dotting the skyline. One of the most notable is the Musée des Confluences, a science and anthropology museum that opened in 2014. The building features a bold and futuristic design that has quickly become one of Lyon's most recognizable landmarks.

In addition to its individual buildings, Lyon's architecture is also shaped by its urban design and planning. The city is known for its traboules, a network of narrow passageways and courtyards that date back to the medieval era. These hidden alleys were originally used by silk merchants to transport their goods and provided a secret network of shortcuts and escape routes.

Lyon's architecture also reflects its status as a major industrial and commercial center. The city's many warehouses, factories, and industrial buildings offer a glimpse into its history as a hub of textile and silk production. Many of these buildings have been repurposed in recent years, with old factories and warehouses transformed into trendy apartments, offices, and cultural spaces.

In conclusion, Lyon's architecture is a rich and diverse tapestry that reflects the city's long and fascinating history. From its Gothic cathedrals and Renaissance palaces to its modern museums and industrial buildings, Lyon's architecture is a testament to its cultural and artistic traditions. Whether exploring the city's historical landmarks or its modern structures, visitors to Lyon are sure to be captivated by its architectural beauty and diversity.

CHAPTER 3: PLANNING YOUR TRIP

After Paris and Marseille, Lyon, the capital of the Rhône-Alpes region in southeast France, is the nation's third-largest city. Lyon, which dates back to the Gallo-Roman era, is currently a significant center for trade, culture, cuisine, and winemaking. Learn how to organize your vacation to Lyon by reading on for information on how to get there, where to stay, what to eat, and what to do.

Planning Your Trip

• The best time to visit Lyon is between mid-spring and late autumn when the weather is milder and excellent for outdoor pursuits like strolling, cycling, and day excursions. You might also think about going in the first few days of December when the city comes to life with Christmas markets, holiday lights, and other activities.

• Language: The dominant tongue of Lyon is French.

• Currency: Since 2002, the Euro has served as France's official unit of account.

• Getting Around: Downtown Lyon and the major tourist attractions are rather small and simple to traverse on foot; make sure you're prepared with either a reliable navigation app on your phone or a printed map. If you want to use public transportation, the city's bus, tram, and metro systems are all reasonably priced. Tickets may be bought at stations or on buses; however, keep in mind that single bus tickets are substantially more expensive than those bought in advance. You may use standard metro/tram tickets or travel passes on the two funicular lines that will take you up the city's two steep slopes. However, local trains depart from downtown Lyon often and effectively for day trips to adjacent vineyards or neighboring cities.

• Travel Tip: If you select a hotel near the main tourist sites, you won't feel like you're in a big city, and you'll save money on transportation.

Things to Do

Whether it's your first or third time to Lyon, which is built up on a mountainous location along the Rhône and Saône rivers2, there is a lot to see and do. It would help if you wandered through the narrow streets of Old Lyon (Vieux Lyon), especially on your first visit. The St-Jean Cathedral, which sits on the western edge of the city, is a stunning example of medieval Gothic architecture, while the warm Italian-style structures in ochre and warm pink were mostly constructed during the Renaissance. Be sure to stroll along

21

the two rivers' banks and over their picturesque bridges. You may even stop for a picnic along the route. Next, enjoy lunch or supper at one of Lyon's famed bouchons, which are classic, often family-owned restaurants known for their straightforward yet delectable regional cuisine.

Many of the best attractions and activities for your visit are listed below:

• Fourvière hill, to the west of Old Lyon, is dominated by Notre-Dame de Fourvière; from the viewing point outside the basilica, you can take in breathtaking panoramic views of the city. Two Roman arena remains may be seen here, along with Lyon's intriguing Gallo-Roman archaeological museum (Musée Lugdunum). A funicular travels to Fourvière and leaves at the foot of the slope in Old Lyon.

• It's been a while since I've done this, but I'm going to try again. Go through the historical passages, or traboules, that formerly allowed silk workers to get products to the city center below as you explore the district of silk weavers on the steep slopes of the region known as La Croix Rousse. 3 It's also worthwhile to explore the Croix-Rousse district itself, which is brimming with amazing street art, unique shops, cafés, and eateries.

• Lyon is a significant historical location for cinema and movies. Learn more about the city's significant contribution to the development of moving pictures by visiting the Lumière Institute and the Museum of Miniatures and Cinema.

What to Eat and Drink

More than 1,000 restaurants may be found in Lyon, which is regarded as France's gourmet capital. In Lyon, you won't have any problem obtaining a satisfying lunch. Traditional, affordable eating options abound in the city, including the bouchons with their cozy dining rooms and genuine atmosphere that was previously described. Tripes, quenelles de brochet (pike fish in a rich, creamy sauce), quenelles de canuts, a soft, herbed "silk weaver's" cheese, and Lyonnais-style salad are some of the regional delicacies. Consider enrolling in a one-day program with Plum Teaching Kitchen Lyon if you want to learn how to prepare dishes using local products.

While you're here, visit the Halles de Lyon Paul Bocuse, a covered market and dining area that bears the late, famous French chef's name. To sample and purchase some fantastic cheeses, fruits, wines, pastries, and distinctive Lyonnais delicacies, browse around 48 busy market booths. In and around the market are some of the best formal and casual dining establishments in the city.

Lyon, which lies in the center of the Rhône wine-producing area, is a great site to sample top-notch French wines, whether you go to a local wine bar or take a day trip to a nearby vineyard or tasting room. On the website of Lyon's Convention and Tourism Bureau, you can find out more about wine excursions in and around the city.

Where to Stay

Lyon, the headquarters of the Rhône-Alpes region and one of the major towns in France, has a huge number of hotels, ranging from well-known international chains to eccentric boutique hotels and B&B-style lodgings. Numerous accommodations falling into the three- and two-star categories provide exceptional value and above-average features. In order to get the greatest deals, be sure to book well in advance if you're visiting from mid-spring to early autumn.

Staying in a furnished vacation rental with a kitchen might be a great way to save costs on dining out if you don't mind cooking some of your meals. You could find yourself in the desire to play with the fresh foods you get regardless, given the abundance of top-notch marketplaces and bakeries in Lyon.

In terms of where to stay in the city, anticipate paying extra per night for hotels in the Presque-île and Vieux Lyon neighborhoods. A little outside of the city center, in places like Perrache (close to the railway station) or Croix-Rousse, prices are often lower. Think about things like how easy it will be to get to the city center by public transportation before making any reservations.

Getting There

The Lyon Saint Exupéry International Airport (LYS), which is 15 miles from the city center, has good connections to the TGV network of France. The Navette Lyon, shuttle bus service connects the airport to the heart of the city as an additional option.

Among the national and low-cost airlines that provide both domestic and international flights to and from LYS are Air France, Austrian Air, Aer Lingus, British Airways, Easyjet, Ryanair, KLM, Emirates, and Lufthansa. You may travel directly from Paris and other major French cities on a number of carriers, including Air France, but if you're coming from North America, you'll often need to connect via Paris-Charles de Gaulle Airport (CDG).

You will arrive at either Part-Dieu or Perrache, two of Lyon's main rail stations if you are traveling by train from another French city or another location in Europe. If you desire to explore the area further, there is a third train station at LYS that might be helpful for moving ahead to cities and villages close to Lyon. The Part-Dieu station is served by TGV trains that frequently run to and from Paris. It is also possible to travel directly between the two major cities on the Eurostar, which runs between London and Lyon and takes around 4 hours and 45 minutes.

Money-Saving Tips

• The Lyon City Card entitles you to free or reduced entry to numerous museums and performances, as well as certain retail discounts. It also grants you unlimited access to the city's bus, metro, tramway, and funicular systems. The Lyon Card is offered as a 24-, 48-, or 72-hour pass, with different prices for adults and kids.

• Think about going to Lyon in the off-season (roughly late October to early April). Flights and hotel accommodations are often more affordable during this time, and you'll also benefit from having the city to yourself more of the time and fewer waits at famous sites.

• There are many free yearly festivals and events held in Lyon, such as the Fête de la Musique (June 21), which offers free musical performances all across the city.

• Lyon's municipal bike program allows you to go about town on two wheels for a reasonable price. Free for the first 30 minutes; reasonable hourly and daily prices afterward.

• The many riverbanks and parks in Lyon may provide the ideal locations for a picnic in the spring and summer. Stock up at one of Lyon's local bakeries or farmers' markets on reasonably priced yet delectable pastries, bread, fruit, and French cheeses.

• Choose to go out for lunch if you want to enjoy Lyon's renowned cuisine while keeping an eye on your budget. Pre-set lunch menus are often substantially less expensive than à la carte supper.

CHAPTER 4: LYON'S MUSEUMS: DISCOVERING ART, HISTORY, AND SCIENCE

Lyon is a city that boasts an impressive array of museums catering to various interests and tastes. Whether you're interested in art, history, or science, a museum in Lyon will surely captivate you.

Art lovers will find plenty to admire in Lyon's many art museums. The Musée des Beaux-Arts is one of the city's most popular cultural attractions, featuring an extensive collection of paintings, sculptures, and decorative arts. The museum's collection includes works by various European masters, from Rubens and Rembrandt to Monet and Picasso. The museum also has a strong collection of ancient Egyptian art and artifacts.

Another must-see for art enthusiasts is the Musée d'Art Contemporain de Lyon, which showcases works by some of our most influential contemporary artists. The museum's collection includes works by Andy Warhol, Damien Hirst, and Takashi Murakami, among others. The museum is also known for its innovative exhibitions and installations, often incorporating multimedia and interactive elements.

History buffs will find plenty to explore in Lyon's many history museums. The Musée Gallo-Romain is one of the city's most important cultural institutions, dedicated to the history and archaeology of the Roman Empire in Lyon and the surrounding region. The museum's collection includes a range of artifacts, from pottery and jewelry to statues and mosaics, offering visitors a fascinating glimpse into life in Roman Lyon.

The Musée de la Résistance et de la Déportation, which details the city's participation in the French Resistance during World War II, is another significant historical institution in Lyon. The museum's collection includes artifacts such as weapons, documents, and personal belongings of Resistance fighters and deportees, as well as powerful testimonies and exhibits highlighting the atrocities committed during the war.

Science enthusiasts will also find plenty to interest them in Lyon's many science museums. The Musée des Confluences is one of the city's most popular cultural attractions, showcasing natural history, anthropology, and science exhibits. The museum's collection includes everything from dinosaur fossils and rare animal specimens to interactive displays on the history of science and technology.

Another science museum worth visiting is the Musée des Automates et des Modèles Réduits, which features a collection of more than 300 automated models and miniatures. The museum's collection includes everything from miniature trains and cars to elaborate mechanical puppets, offering visitors a fascinating look at the history and technology of automation.

Lyon also boasts several museums that offer visitors a unique and immersive experience. One such museum is the Musée Miniature et Cinéma, which showcases a collection of over 100 miniature film sets and special effects props used in famous movies. Visitors can explore these detailed miniature sets and learn the techniques used to create movie magic.

Another immersive museum experience can be found at the Musée des Confluences, which features several interactive exhibits that allow visitors to explore the natural world and learn about scientific concepts hands-on. The museum's "Origins" exhibit, for example, takes visitors on a journey through the universe's history, from the Big Bang to the present day.

In conclusion, Lyon's museums offer a wealth of cultural, historical, and scientific treasures for visitors to explore. Whether you're interested in art, history, or science or want to experience something unique and immersive, Lyon has a museum that is sure to captivate you. From ancient Roman artifacts and world-renowned works of art to cutting-edge science exhibits and elaborate miniature sets, Lyon's museums are a testament to the city's rich cultural and artistic traditions.

Best and top Museums in Lyon

Lyon is a city of cultural and historical significance, and its museums offer visitors a glimpse into the city's rich and diverse past. From art and history to science and technology, Lyon's museums cater to a range of interests and are a must-see for anyone visiting the city. Here are some of the best and top museums to explore in Lyon:

1.   Musée des Beaux-Arts de Lyon

The Musée des Beaux-Arts de Lyon is one of the most important art museums in France and boasts an extensive collection of paintings, sculptures, and decorative arts. Rembrandt, Rubens, Monet, and Van Gogh are just a few of the most well-known painters whose works are in the museum's collection. The museum's permanent collection is shown over 70 rooms of a stunning 17th-century structure that was formerly a Benedictine monastery. Visitors can also enjoy temporary exhibitions and events held throughout the year.

2.   Musée d'Art Contemporain de Lyon

The Musée d'Art Contemporain de Lyon is a must-see for contemporary art lovers. Some of the most significant contemporary artists of our day, such as Andy Warhol, Damien Hirst, and Takashi Murakami, have pieces in the museum's collection. The museum is also known for its innovative exhibitions and installations, which often incorporate multimedia and interactive elements. The building itself is also an architectural marvel, with a striking glass and steel façade that reflects the surrounding landscape.

3.   Musée des Confluences

The Musée des Confluences is a science museum located at the confluence of the Rhône and Saône rivers. The museum's collection includes exhibits on natural history, anthropology, and science and features everything from dinosaur fossils and rare animal specimens to interactive displays on the history of science and technology. The museum's architecture is also a work of art, with a bold, contemporary design that has won numerous awards.

4.   Musée Gallo-Romain de Lyon

The Musée Gallo-Romain de Lyon is dedicated to the history and archaeology of the Roman Empire in Lyon and the surrounding region. The museum's collection includes a range of artifacts, from pottery and jewelry to statues and mosaics, offering visitors a fascinating glimpse into life in Roman Lyon. The museum is housed in a beautiful 20th-century building that was designed to resemble an ancient Roman villa, and its permanent collection is spread across three floors.

5.   Musée des Automates et des Modèles Réduits

The Musée des Automates et des Modèles Réduits is a museum dedicated to the history and technology of automation. The museum's collection includes more than 300 automated models and miniatures, including miniature trains and cars, elaborate mechanical puppets, and working model steam engines. The museum is housed in a beautiful 19th-century building that was originally a textile factory, and visitors can also enjoy the museum's impressive collection of antique dolls and toys.

6.   Musée Miniature et Cinéma

The Musée Miniature et Cinéma is a unique museum that showcases a collection of over 100 miniature film sets and special effects props used in famous movies. Visitors can explore these detailed miniature sets and learn about the techniques used to create movie magic. The museum also features exhibits on the history of cinema and special effects, and visitors can even try their hand at creating their own special effects using green screen technology.

7.   Musée Lumière

The Musée Lumière is a museum dedicated to the history and technology of cinema. The museum is housed in the former home of the Lumière family, who is credited with inventing the motion picture camera in the late 19th century. The museum's collection includes a range of artifacts related to the Lumière family's contribution to cinema, including cameras, projectors, and original film prints. The museum also features interactive exhibits and screenings of classic films, making it a must-see for film enthusiasts.

8.   Musée de l'Imprimerie et de la Communication Graphique

The history of printing and graphic design is the focus of the Musée de l'Imprimerie et de la Communication Graphique. The museum's collection includes a range of printing presses and equipment, as well as rare books, manuscripts, and posters. Visitors can learn about the evolution of printing technology and its impact on communication and media. The museum also offers workshops and demonstrations on printing techniques, making it a great place for both adults and children.

9.   Musée des Tissus et des Arts Décoratifs

The Musée des Tissus et des Arts Décoratifs is a museum dedicated to the history and production of textiles and decorative arts. The museum's collection includes fabrics, costumes, and furnishings from the Middle Ages to the present day, as well as a collection of Asian textiles and decorative arts. Visitors can explore the museum's extensive collection and learn about the techniques and traditions of textile production throughout history.

10.   Musée Tony Garnier

The Musée Tony Garnier is dedicated to the life and work of the famous architect and urban planner Tony Garnier. The museum features a collection of Garnier's original plans and drawings, as well as photographs and models of his most famous works, including the "Cité Industrielle" project, which aimed to create an ideal industrial city. Visitors can learn about Garnier's vision for urban planning and his contribution to Lyon's urban development.

Overall, Lyon's museums offer a diverse range of exhibits and collections that cater to a variety of interests. Whether you're a fan of art, history, science, or technology, Lyon's museums are sure to provide an unforgettable experience. So, make sure to include these top museums on your itinerary when visiting this beautiful city.

Best Shopping Malls in Lyon

Lyon is a city with a rich history and culture, but it also offers visitors a great shopping experience. The city boasts several modern and trendy shopping malls that cater to all tastes and budgets. We will showcase Lyon's top retail centers in this area, so you know where to go.

1.   Confluence Shopping Center

The Confluence Shopping Center is a modern and spacious mall located in the heart of Lyon's Confluence district. The mall features over 220 stores, including international and French brands, such as H&M, Zara, and Sephora. Moreover, there are several dining options, a movie theater, and a children's indoor playground. The mall's unique architecture, with its glass facades and open spaces, provides a pleasant shopping experience.

2.   Part-Dieu Shopping Center

The Part-Dieu Shopping Center is one of Lyon's largest and most popular malls, located in the Part-Dieu district. The mall features over 260 stores, ranging from high-end fashion brands to electronics and home decor. There are also several restaurants and cafes, as well as a cinema and an ice-skating rink. The mall's central location, close to the Part-Dieu train station, makes it easily accessible.

3.   La Part Dieu Shopping Mall

La Part Dieu Shopping Mall is located in the heart of Lyon's business district and is one of the city's largest shopping centers. With more than 250 shops, including flagship stores for major French and international brands such as FNAC, H&M, and Zara, the mall offers a great selection of fashion, accessories, and electronics. The mall also has a number of restaurants and cafes, including a food court, a cinema complex, and an ice-skating rink.

4.   Carre de Soie Shopping Center

The Carre de Soie Shopping Center is a modern and vibrant mall located in the Vaulx-en-Velin district of Lyon. The mall features over 120 stores, including fashion, beauty, and electronics brands. There are also several restaurants and cafes, as well as a cinema and a bowling alley. The mall's unique design, with its colorful facades and green spaces, provides a fun and inviting atmosphere for shoppers.

5.   Grand'Place Shopping Center

The Grand'Place Shopping Center is a large and modern mall located in the Sainte-Genevieve-des-Bois district of Lyon. The mall features over 100 stores, including fashion, beauty, and electronics brands, as well as several restaurants and cafes. The mall also has a cinema and a bowling alley, making it a great destination for a day out with friends or family.

6.   Lyon Part Dieu Shopping Mall

The Lyon Part Dieu Shopping Mall is located in the heart of the city, next to the Part-Dieu train station. The mall features over 260 stores, including high-end fashion brands, electronics stores, and home decor shops. There are also several restaurants and cafes, as well as a cinema complex and an ice-skating rink. The mall's central location and easy access make it a convenient destination for both locals and tourists.

7.   Centre Commercial Auchan Porte des Alpes

The Centre Commercial Auchan Porte des Alpes is a large and modern mall located in the Saint-Priest district of Lyon. The mall features over 150 stores, including fashion, electronics, and home decor brands. There are also several restaurants and cafes, as well as a cinema and a bowling alley. The mall's spacious layout and modern design provide a comfortable and enjoyable shopping experience.

In conclusion, Lyon offers a great shopping experience with its modern and trendy shopping malls. From high-end fashion to electronics and home decor, there is something for everyone. So, whether you're a fashion enthusiast, tech geek, or just looking for a fun day out, Lyon's shopping malls are sure to satisfy your needs. The malls also offer a variety of dining options and entertainment activities, making them ideal destinations for a day out with friends or family.

It's worth noting that Lyon also has several street markets and boutique shops that offer a unique and authentic shopping experience. Les Puces du Canal, for example, is a popular flea market located in the Villeurbanne district, where you can find vintage clothing, antiques, and other unique items. The Croix-Rousse district is also known for its silk boutiques, where you can find high-quality silk scarves, ties, and other accessories.

In addition to shopping, Lyon has a lot to offer in terms of culture, history, and gastronomy. So, make sure to take some time to explore the city's museums, historical landmarks, and famous culinary scenes while you're here.

In conclusion, Lyon's shopping malls offer a great selection of stores, dining options, and entertainment activities. Whether you're looking for luxury fashion brands or affordable electronics, Lyon has it all. So, add these malls to your itinerary and enjoy a fun and memorable shopping experience in one of France's most beautiful cities.

CHAPTER 5: LYON'S NEIGHBORHOODS: EXPLORING THE CITY'S DIFFERENT DISTRICTS

Lyon is a city with a rich history and diverse culture, and each of its neighborhoods has a unique character and charm. From the winding streets of Vieux Lyon to the trendy bars of Croix-Rousse, there's something for everyone in Lyon's various districts. Let's examine some of Lyon's most renowned neighborhoods in more detail.

1.   Vieux Lyon: Located on the west bank of the Saône River, Vieux Lyon is the city's historic district and one of its most popular tourist destinations. Its narrow streets are lined with Renaissance-era buildings and traboules, or secret passageways, that connect the different buildings. The district is home to many landmarks, including the Gothic-style Cathédrale Saint-Jean-Baptiste and the Musée Gadagne, which houses Lyon's history and puppetry museums.

2.   Presqu'île: This district is located between the Rhône and Saône rivers and is the commercial and

financial center of Lyon. Its wide avenues are lined with high-end fashion boutiques, department stores, and restaurants. Presqu'île is also home to many of Lyon's cultural landmarks, including the Opéra de Lyon and the Musée des Beaux-Arts.

3.   Croix-Rousse: Located on a hill overlooking the city, Croix-Rousse is known for its bohemian atmosphere and vibrant nightlife. The district was once the center of Lyon's silk industry and is home to many silk boutiques and workshops. Croix-Rousse also has a thriving arts scene, with many galleries and performance spaces.

4.   La Confluence: This district is located at the southern tip of Presqu'île and is Lyon's newest neighborhood. La Confluence was once an industrial area but has been transformed into a modern and sustainable urban space. Its sleek buildings, including the Musée des Confluences and the Orange Cube, house cultural and commercial spaces.

5.   Guillotière: Located on the east bank of the Rhône River, Guillotière is a diverse and multicultural neighborhood. Its vibrant streets are lined with shops and restaurants serving cuisine from around the world. Guillotière is also home to many cultural landmarks,

including the Musée des Arts Africains, Océaniens, Amérindiens and the Institut Lumière, which celebrates the history of cinema.

6.   Fourvière: Located on a hill overlooking the city, Fourvière is home to Lyon's most famous landmark, the Basilique Notre-Dame de Fourvière. The district is also home to the Roman-era Théâtre Antique and the Musée Gallo-Romain, which houses artifacts from Lyon's Roman past. The district has stunning views of the city and is a popular spot for picnics and outdoor activities.

In conclusion, Lyon's neighborhoods offer a diverse range of experiences, from exploring the city's history and culture to indulging in its culinary delights and vibrant nightlife. So, make sure to take some time to explore each of these unique districts and discover all that Lyon has to offer.

A Map of Lyon's Neighborhoods

One of the biggest and most significant cities in France, Lyon, is home to various districts and neighborhoods, each of which has unique attractions. Be careful to get familiar with Lyon's nine arrondissements (districts), labeled 1 through 9, while arriving for the first time. Knowing them before your trip can make navigating the city easier and help you decide what to prioritize among the city's top attractions. For a summary of each neighborhood's highlights, continue reading.

1: Place des Terreaux & City Hall

The 1st arrondissement makes up a large portion of the current city center of Lyon and is home to several attractions significant to local culture and tourists. The location is south of the Croix-Rousse district (4th arrondissement), southwest of Old Lyon, and north of Fourviere on the Presqu'ile, a natural island between the Rhone and Saone rivers. The most convenient station on the Metro lines A and C serving the region is Hôtel de Ville-Louis Pradel.

Steps to Take: The opulent Plaza des Terreaux, home to neoclassical structures, a Bartholdi fountain, the Fine Arts Museum, eateries, and crowded café terraces, serves as the neighborhood's hub. The elaborate 17th-century City Hall is on the square's east side. See the Lyon Opera, which was constructed by architect Jean Nouvel and combines a 19th-century foundation with a modern, domed rooftop.

2: Place Bellecour & Confluences

Extending from the lower section of the Presqu'ile between Lyon's two rivers, southward to the Confluences region where the Rhone and Saone meet, the 2nd arrondissement encompasses a busy part of the city center, filled with commercial areas, a spectacular plaza, restaurants, theaters, and amazingly various architectural styles. To get there, take Metro Line A to Cordeliers or Perrache, two of the city's main train/TGV stations.

Steps to Take: Start in the vast Place Bellecour, which is also Europe's biggest plaza and has a monument of Louis XIV, known as the "Sun King," riding a horse. From here, visit the international stores, cafés, and restaurants that line streets like Rue de la Republique and Rue Victor Hugo. One of France's oldest theaters, the Theatre des Celestins, is located on the captivating Place des Celestins. Next, go south to the Musee des Confluences to see its futuristic architecture and natural history exhibitions.

3: Part Dieu and Les Halles Market

The 3rd arrondissement in Lyon may not be the most attractive area, but it has a lot to offer visitors from outside, particularly those who are interested in local cuisine, wine, and markets. The region sometimes referred to as Lyon's second city center and home to the bustling Part-Dieu railway station is situated directly east of the Presque'ile across the Rhone. With commercial complexes, one of France's top-covered food markets, and a buzzing, modern ambiance, it serves as a fantastic hub for travelers entering or leaving Lyon. Many metro and tram lines service the neighborhood, and the Rhoneexpress airport tram/shuttle also stops at Part-Dieu.

What to Do: Set aside a few hours to browse the Halles de Lyon-Paul Bocuse, a covered market with hundreds of booths offering everything from fresh local fruit to cheeses, bread, chocolate, and wines. The market is named after the late and renowned chef. The market is surrounded by a ton of excellent eateries. While waiting, walk with city views along the Berges du Rhône or stop for a drink on the rooftop of a peniche (boat cafe/bar).

4: Croix-Rousse

The Croix-Rousse (4th arrondissement), located north of the city center in the first district, is one of Lyon's most vibrant and artistic districts, fusing the city's industrial past with present-day local life. The area formerly contained many silk workers' workshops, as indicated by the passages (traboules) that link the buildings to the city center and allow employees to carry materials and products to market. Lyon was once a major hub for the production of silk. From the Fourvière district, you may either walk there or take Metro line C to the Croix-Rousse station.

Steps to Take: Start your exploration of the area's twisting alleyways, panoramic vistas, and bustling, laid-back cafés, boutiques, and restaurants at the Place de la Croix Rousse. The area resembles an autonomous community in many aspects. Be sure to see the Theatre de la Croix-Rousse, a theater with a magnificent 1920s exterior, and other famous locations like the Mur des Canuts, a dizzying trompe-l'oeil mural that depicts the history of the region's silk weavers.

5: Fourviere and Old Lyon

The 5th arrondissement extends along the left bank of the Saone River into the high heights of Fourvière Basilica, serving as the historical center of both Gallo-Roman and medieval Lyon. Most visitors will want to spend a significant amount of time here since it is brimming with well-known sites, stunning architecture, and magnificent city vistas. Metro line D makes it quite simple to get there (Vieux Lyon station).

What to Do: After seeing the Saint-Jean Church from the 12th century, stroll through the twisting alleyways dotted with eateries and stores, admire the lovely bridges across the Saone River, and take in the warm hues of the Renaissance-era buildings of Vieux Lyon with their hidden tunnels (traboules). Then ride one of the two funicular trains to the top of Fourviere hill to visit the Basilica, its sweeping vistas, the Gallo-Roman museum, and the historical arenas.

6: Parc de la Tete d'Or

The 6th arrondissement is a rich area that is mostly residential. It is located on the right bank of the Rhone River, northeast of the city center, and to the north of the 3rd arrondissement and the Halles de Lyon/Part Dieu district. The 6th provides elegance and fresh air thanks to its abundance of mansions and residential structures from the 18th century, as well as the city's biggest central park and majestic footbridges spanning the Rhone. To reach there via public transportation, use Metro Line A to the Foch or Massena stations.

What to Do: Go north to the Park de la Tete d'Or, France's biggest urban green area, after crossing one of the bridges across the Rhone into the 6th (the Passerelle du College footbridge gives particularly stunning views). The lovely park has enough grass for a leisurely picnic, tree-lined pathways and walking routes, artificial lakes, and caves.

7: University District & Parc Blandan

The progressive 7th arrondissement, one of Lyon's most recent neighborhoods, is home to numerous colleges, some of whose grand buildings look out over the Rhône River and its green-lined walking and cycling routes. It is located southeast of the city's core. It is readily accessible by Metro or on foot from downtown Place Bellecour (crossing the Bridge de la Guillotière) (Line B or C).

Steps to Take: Discover the relaxed student atmosphere, cafés, and variety of street food choices in the University District, which is located between Rue de Chevreul and Rue de Marseille. Although the verdant Parc Blandan is another of the city's most beautiful green areas, the riverfront route along the Berges du Rhone provides kilometers of walking and cycling pathways. The Centre d'Histoire de la Resistance et de la Deportation (CHRD), a museum and memorial space that examines Lyon's history during World War II, should be your last destination.

8: Institut Lumiere

East of the city's core, the 8th arrondissement is a bustling, historically working-class neighborhood bounded by the 7th and 3rd districts. One of Lyon's more recent neighborhoods, it has a modern, diversified air. It offers great transportation options to the city (via Metro Line D or Tram Line T2 at the Sans-Souci and Monplaisir-Lumiere stations). Budget-conscious guests will find the lodging here typically more affordable than in the city center.

Steps to Take: The Institut de Lumiere, which houses a collection centered on the development of cinema and the contributions made by the Lumiere brothers, natives of Lyon and pioneers of the industry, is a must-visit for movie buffs and cinephiles. It is located in the Montplaisir neighborhood.

9: Ile Barbe and Place Valmy

The 9th arrondissement, a residential and green neighborhood perched above Old Lyon and next to the Croix-Rousse neighborhood, is about 4 miles northwest of the city center (4th arrondissement). It provides effective public transportation connections to Lyons' top sights (from Metro Line D at Gorge de Loup, Valmy, and Gare de Vaise stations). It can be a nice alternative if you want to experience local life quietly or are searching for affordable lodging.

Steps to Take: A 5th-century monastery is located on the Ile Barbe, a natural island in the Saône home to attractive riverside walking and bicycling pathways along the banks of the Saone. The Place de Valmy neighborhood, with its shops, eateries, and convenient access to the riverfront walkways, is well worth a brief visit. From here, you can take the Metro into the city center.

CHAPTER 6: PUBLIC TRANSIT IN LYON: GETTING AROUND

Lyon is one of France's largest and most significant cities, yet it's still rather simple to get about. Most tourist attractions are located in or close to the city center, and the public transit system in Lyon is effective and simple. Learn about the city's public transportation choices before you come. Investigate ticket prices and travel passes; depending on how long you stay, how much you can see on foot, and the attractions you want, some alternatives will make more sense than others. Make a plan in advance to travel with ease.

How to Ride the Metro

As a tourist, the Lyon Metro system is your best bet for traveling from one place to the next. The Metro, which has four lines and connects the city's core and neighboring suburbs, provides service to several well-known locations, including Vieux Lyon (Old Lyon), Place Bellecour and the Presqu'île neighborhood, Hôtel de Ville (City Hall), and the Croix-Rousse region. Moreover, it connects to Lyon-Part Dieu and Perrache, the city's two rails and TGV (high-speed train) stations. Moreover, two funicular lines leave from Vieux Lyon.

• Operating Hours: The Metro is open daily from 5 a.m. to 12 a.m.

• Routes: Due to their frequent stops at the attractions above and a wide variety of additional areas of interest, Metro Lines C and D are the most helpful for travelers. Also, the F1 and F2 funicular lines provide a fantastic (and endearingly retro) way to ascend the steep slope from Old Lyon to the ancient Roman arenas and Gallo-Roman Museum or Fourvière, with its basilica and panoramic vistas.   .

• Tickets and Fares: Metrocards may be used on buses, tramways, and the two funicular lines in addition to the Metro. Currently, a single ticket costs 1.90 euros when bought at a station or approved dealer. (If bought on the bus, the ticket will cost 2.20 euros.) During an hour, one ticket is good for one free transfer (round journey). However, the ticket has to be confirmed each time. Currently, 10-ticket booklets cost 17.60 euros, and a 24-hour unlimited day pass costs 3.20 euros. Last but not least, single funicular tickets are presently 3 euros for a roundtrip on any funicular line.

Riding the Tram

Another practical transportation option in Lyon is its tramway system, although as it mostly serves the city's periphery and neighboring suburbs, it isn't very helpful for visiting the city's top tourist destinations. The tram may be a useful alternative, however, if you want to save money by staying in a more sedate, residential neighborhood or need to go from the nearby airport to the railway station fast. Tram rides are covered by the Lyon City Card, and the ticketing procedure is the same as for metro trains, buses, and buses.

Seven tram lines in all (T1, T2, T3, T4, T5, T6, and T7) are available, in addition to the Rhône Express, which links Lyon Part-Dieu station and Saint-Exupéry Airport. They run from 5 a.m. (some as early as 4:30 a.m.) to around 12:30 a.m. every day. The T1 line, which travels north to south and has stations at places like the University of Lyon, the Lyon-Perrache railway station, the Parc de la Tête d'Or park, and the Musée des Confluences, is perhaps the handiest for tourists.

Keep in mind that pedestrians may want to avoid places near tramway rails. While on or near tracks, be cautious of any incoming trams: Search both directions and keep an eye out for any signs that a tram crossing is about to occur.

Riding the Bus

Although using the bus on your journey to Lyon may not be required, they may be helpful sometimes. They are a convenient, pleasant method of transportation for certain tourists, particularly those who have restricted mobility, and because of their extensive coverage, you may use them practically anyplace. The city, its suburbs, and the nearby villages are all served by more than 100 bus and trolley bus routes. There are additional night bus services available.

Check out the TCL network's timetables and routes if you believe you may want to or need to use the bus in Lyon or use the convenient English trip planner (probably the best option for visitors). If in doubt, plan your route using Google Maps or another navigation tool.

Purchase and Usage of Tickets

At the majority of metro, tram, and railway (rail) stations in Lyon, including Lyon-Part Dieu and Perrache stations, you may buy tickets for the city's Metro, bus, tram, and funicular lines. Moreover, tickets are offered for sale in tabacs (tobacco dispensers/convenience shops), TCL agencies located around the city, and tourist information offices. Cash or credit cards may be used to buy bus tickets onboard, but be advised that they are somewhat more expensive than when purchased in advance from automated kiosks or approved points of sale.

Before each travel, make careful to verify your bus, tram, funicular, or metro tickets or passes by inserting them into the digital readers. You may use them for up to an hour after validation, and you are free to make as many transfers as necessary between buses, trams, funiculars, and metro lines during that time. Keep in mind that breaking any of these regulations or attempting to use a ticket after it has expired may result in fines.

Renting a car

It is often not required to hire a vehicle in Lyon if your primary goal is to explore the city. Only if you want to make multiple-day journeys, such as to surrounding wine-producing regions and towns (including Beaujolais) or to locations in the French Alps, do we advise you to take into account renting a vehicle (Annecy, Grenoble). Use the Park and Ride service if you decide to hire a vehicle rather than drive through the city center to save stress and traffic. Before getting behind the wheel, be careful to educate yourself about French traffic rules.

Traveling to and from the Airport via Public Transportation

Using public transportation from Lyon Airport to the city center is a rather simple and short process. The simplest approach is to go from the airport to the Lyon-Part Dieu station on the Rhône Express tram route (or the inverse). You may take a bus or a metro train into the city center from Part Dieu. Shuttle buses may take you from any terminal to the tram, which departs from the SNCF train station. Each way, the journey takes slightly under 30 minutes. Tickets may be purchased immediately at the airport or in most stations, or in advance on the Rhône Express website.

You may also take a cab to and from the airport but be advised that this is a far more costly alternative, with one-way prices right now costing anything from 45 to 55 euros to get from the city center to the airport.

Tips for Getting Around Lyon

• Think about purchasing the Lyon City Card, which comes with benefits like unlimited rides on all tram, bus, and funicular lines, cheap admission to a number of well-liked sites in Lyon, a sightseeing cruise, a tour with a guide from the tourist office, and more. There is discounted pricing for students and children under the age of 14, and you may choose cards that are good for 24, 48, or 72 hours.

• Keep in mind that the Lyon Metro operates until 1 a.m. if you want to enjoy some nightlife and remain out beyond midnight. There are night buses; however, they could be a little difficult for visitors to understand. Consider getting a cab if you're out late and your hotel is too far to go there on foot to prevent a headache or possible security issues.

• Except for transportation to or from the airport or late-night trips, it's typically better to avoid utilizing taxis in Lyon. Because of traffic, fares are often fairly expensive, particularly throughout the day.

• If you want to go on a day excursion but don't have access to a vehicle, think about signing up for a shuttle or van tour that will transport you to surrounding towns and wineries.

• All public transit in Lyon is free for children under the age of four. Groups of 10 or more may also purchase tickets at a reduced rate.

• If you can, we advise traveling mostly on foot during the warmer months, particularly if you decide to stay in the city center. But remember to carry a sturdy pair of walking shoes and to drink enough water on hot days.

• The city's bike rental program is both reasonably priced and simple to use, and certain parts of Lyon, such as those along the riverbanks, may be great for a bike ride. The tourist information center also suggests a number of electric bike excursions, which might be an excellent way to see the city outside.

• Visitors with impairments related to poor mobility, eyesight, or hearing may often use Lyon's public transportation system without much difficulty. All trams and buses are equipped with ramps or level access points to make them accessible to riders in wheelchairs or with restricted mobility. With the exception of Croix-Paquet, all metro stations include escalators, elevators with ramps, braille displays, audio announcements, and accessible methods of the entrance to train platforms. Visit the Facilities Information Service for further information.

CHAPTER 7: HOW TO TRAVEL BY RAIL, BUS, CAR, AND AIRLINE FROM PARIS TO LYON

Lyon, the second-largest city in France (after Paris, of course), is home to several historical and architectural masterpieces, earning it the prestigious designation of a UNESCO World Heritage Site. One of the most vibrant towns in France, Lyon is also known as the top gourmet center of the nation, as seen by the few brasseries from the great Paul Bocuse, it is home to, not to mention those region-specific bouchons.

There is lots of medieval and Renaissance architecture, but the cuisine alone makes the trip worthwhile. While it only attracts a few foreign visitors as Paris sometimes does, this is one of its charms. Here, in a less hectic environment, you may experience real French culture. Paris and Lyon are separated by a driving distance of 288 miles and a flying distance of 244 miles (393 kilometers) (463 kilometers). More frequently than not, people choose to drive between the two cities, making stops in Burgundy and other places along the route. Yet, the direct train takes half the time.

How to Get From Paris to Lyon

• Flight: one hour, from $100

• Train: beginning at $65 for 2 hours (fastest)

• Driving: 288 miles in 4 hours and 30 minutes (463 kilometers)

• Bus: beginning at $16 for six hours (slowest, but potentially the cheapest)

By Plane

The time-consuming element is traveling to and from airports; the trip from Paris to Lyon only lasts around an hour. The main (and least expensive) airport serving Paris is Charles de Gaulle, which is situated 35 kilometers (22 miles) outside of the city. With an hour-long trip and a 30-minute fast train journey from Lyon Airport to get there, it might take anything between 30 and an hour to get there. You can take the train and still have time to check into your hotel room in the time it takes to fly.

Nevertheless, if flying is more your style, you should be fine with getting a ticket as there are more than 500 weekly direct flights between Paris and Lyon. There are seven direct flights, the most popular of which is Air France. During the off-peak months of February through April, one-way tickets cost around $100. Nevertheless, during busy travel periods (almost all other times of the year, but notably in January), airfare costs soar to $200 or more. The most costly and most definitely not the quickest choice is this one.

By train

In terms of public transit, trains are the quickest and most widely used means of transportation. As the TGV travels at a speed of 186 miles (300 kilometers) per hour, which is almost three times as quickly as a vehicle would, it only takes two hours to go from Paris Gare De Lyon to Lyon Part Dieu. Almost every hour of the day, trains depart from this conveniently located station in the Place Louis Armand (Paris' 12th arrondissement). Costs for tickets range from $65 to $130.

By Car

The benefits and drawbacks of driving your own vehicle (or a rental car). Indeed, having the option to spend a night in locations like Burgundy, Dijon, or Geneva is very precious, but for someone who is unfamiliar with the region, leaving Paris might be a nightmare.

There are a few routes that will get you from point A to point B, depending on whether you want to make a detour to the Ardeche or the Alps, but the most direct one will take you there in around four and a half hours. The distance from Paris to Lyon is 288 miles (463 kilometers).

Take the A6 to Exit A6B toward Lyon from the heart of Paris. Up until Exit 39B, which will take you directly into Lyon's center, nearly entirely follow the A6.

By Bus

The bus isn't usually the first option since it takes the longest (approximately six hours), but if you manage to get a ticket for $16, it could be the most affordable option. Even at $40, tickets are still less expensive than riding the train. The FlixBus, the BlaBlaBus, or the Eurolines FR, which leave from Bercy Station in the center at all hours of the day and night, are better options for budget travelers with more time to spare if they want to save a few dollars. By boarding an overnight bus (11:30 p.m. to 5:30 a.m.) rather than paying for a hostel or hotel room, you may save even more money.

What to See in Lyon

The third-largest city in France, established over 2,000 years ago, is rich in culture and the past. You may spend as much time exploring the city's streets or relaxing in one of the numerous parks as there are museums, historical structures, and wonderful restaurants.

The Vieux Lyon neighborhood's Cathédrale Saint-Jean-Baptiste is a well-liked tourist destination. You may pass away an afternoon dancing to the buskers that frequent this area of the city, known as Fourvière, where the magnificent Basilica of Notre-Dame de Fourvière, which towers above the city, lies on a hill overlooking it. Another large area is Place Bellecour, where you may get lost in the throng while chowing down on a pastrami sandwich or one of those mouthwatering street crepes.

Speaking about cuisine, this city is renowned for its traditional, homey cuisine. It is a good idea to have a backup plan in place in case the backup plan fails. Going during lunch instead of supper might help you save a little money. The best restaurants often offer set meals for as little as $20 in the afternoon. Drinks are dominated by artisan coffee and mixology.

Get some fresh air in Park de la Tête d'Or, a large park in the middle with sculptures and plants, after your midday excesses. Perhaps visit the Gallo-Roman Museum of Lyon-Fourvière or the Museum of Fine Arts, two top-notch institutions.

CHAPTER 8: TOP 20 ACTIVITIES IN LYON, FRANCE

One of France's most populated and intriguing towns, Lyon is located in the verdant Rhône Valley. Over two thousand years old, the ancient Gallo-Roman city is home to world-famous local food and wines and offers interested tourists a variety of intriguing attractions, including museums and secret tunnels. Find out more about the top attractions of the city once called "Lugdunum" by reading on.

1. Discover Vieux Lyon (Old Town)

Vieux Lyon, 69005 Lyon, France

The greatest place to start any first visit is Vieux Lyon, often known as Old Town. It was built in the early Middle Ages, but now its well-preserved Renaissance structures make it noteworthy.

Through cobblestone streets, Old Town runs parallel to the Saône River from north to south. It is tucked up against Fourvière Hill, which is home to some of the city's most exquisite buildings from the 15th and 16th centuries. These structures are renowned for their Italian Renaissance-styled rose- and orange-hued façades.

Get off at the Vieux Lyon-St Jean metro station to begin your exploration of the neighborhood's winding streets, small boutiques, historic eateries, and covert courtyards. The area's major thoroughfare for eating and shopping is Rue Saint-Jean.

2. Admire the Architecture at Saint-Jean Cathedral

Pl. Saint-Jean, 69005 Lyon, France

The Saint-Jean Cathedral, which was finished in 1480, is a true masterpiece. At the southern end of Old Lyon, it overlooks Place Saint-Jean, a UNESCO World Heritage Site.

The Cathedral's eclectic architectural design represents the many stages of its long-term development. The Gothic-style nave and façade of Saint-Jean were added later, while the apse and choir were created in the Romanesque style.

A magnificent rose stained-glass window from the 12th century, an astronomical clock that was installed in the 14th, and sculptures adorning the façade that depict biblical tales are some of the building's further notable features. See the Bourbon chapel as well; it was constructed in the 15th century by the Duke of Bourbon and is renowned for its intricate sculptures.

3. Lyon's Traboules (Old Passageways)

See the various traboules of the city for a fascinating look at Lyonnai's history. There are several Renaissance-era structures on Fourvière hill that are connected by these networks of ramped, covered, or partially covered passages. Some are believed to have existed as far back as the fourth century, while others were added in later decades.

Despite the fact that many traboules were probably constructed so that locals could easily descend from their residences to the ancient town below, others were given new uses in the 19th century. They made it possible for silk weavers to get fabrics down the steep slope to reach merchants by linking the Croix Rousse neighborhood's silk industry to the Vieux Lyon commercial district. Later, during World War Two, French Resistance members made a name for themselves by planning meetings and hiding from Gestapo officials in the corridors, something many outsiders were unaware of.

To visit some of the most magnificent traboules and admire architectural elements like elaborate galleries and dizzying spiral stairs, we advise having a guided tour of the traboules.

4. Gallo-Roman Museum & Arenas (Musée Lugdunum)

17 Rue Cleberg, 69005 Lyon, France

PHONE +33 4 72 38 49 30

This museum and archaeological site reveal Lyon's significance throughout the Roman Empire, adding to the city's magnificent layers of medieval and Renaissance legacy.

A museum rich with Gallo-Roman relics and everyday items is part of the UNESCO World Heritage site, which is perched on the precipitous slopes of Fourvière near two impressive Roman amphitheaters. At its peak, the main amphitheater, which is the biggest in France, could accommodate 10,000 spectators for plays and other performances. The "Odeon" arena, which had a capacity of around 3,000, was presumably utilized for political gatherings and performances. Even today, open-air summer concerts and other events are held in the arenas.

Also, there are on-site Roman baths, chapels, rose gardens, and panoramic city views for visitors to enjoy.

5. Fourvière Basilica for a Panoramic View of the City

8 Pl. de Fourvière, 69005 Lyon, France

Phone: +33 4 78 25 13 01

The Fourvière Basilica (Basilique Notre Dame de Fourvière in French), which is sometimes likened to Sacré

Coeur in Paris, is majestically atop the hill with the same name and provides stunning views of Lyon's landmarks and roofs.

The brilliant white Basilica, built in 1884, combines Roman and Byzantine architectural styles. It was constructed as a symbol of protection in the wake of the bubonic plague that ravaged Europe in the 17th century and is dedicated to the Virgin Mary.

Although some consider Fourvière to be a representation of Lyon itself, others find its design offensive and liken it to an "upside-down elephant." See the outside and the golden interiors before soaking in the expansive vistas of the city, regardless of your opinion of the building's architectural qualities.

6. Lyonnais "Bouchon"

Lyon is renowned for its gastronomy and cuisine. Visit one of its bouchons for a genuine taste of some of the greatest at a fair price. These cozy, traditional restaurants provide imaginative cuisine from local cooks as well as regional delicacies like pike quenelles and Charolais meat.

Le Bouchon des Cordeliers or Café du Peintre are two options if you're seeking a dining spot that combines tradition with creative menu items.

7. Learn About Lyon's Puppeteering and Marionette-Making Traditions

1 Pl. du Petit Collège, 69005 Lyon, France

PHONE +33 4 78 42 03 61

The twin collection at Musées Gadagne explores the city's puppeteering and marionette-making traditions while also providing further insight into Lyon's lengthy history.

Visit the history museum to discover more about Lyon during the Renaissance. You may research the period's everyday activities, artistic and cultural accomplishments, architecture, and more.

All ages will appreciate the vintage yet entertaining collection at the Puppet Museum. Read more about the odd, adorable local practice of presenting elaborate puppet plays that even adults flock to, as well as the traditional creation of wooden marionettes (also known as guignols in French).

8. Taste & Stroll at Lyon's Famous Food Market

69003 Lyon, France

This market, which first opened its doors in 1859, should be your main priority while visiting Lyon. Halles de Lyon, Les Paul Bocuse is named after one of France's most renowned chefs and provides foodies with a labyrinth of pleasures spread over around fifty kiosks.

A vast selection of genuine French cheeses, baked items, herbs, sauces, chocolate, vibrant fruit from surrounding farms, and more can be found here. Shops like Maison Malartre provide everything from Lyonnais quenelles (pike dumplings) to escargot and decadent sauces if you want to explore or purchase regional delicacies.

If the weather permits, come to stock up on food for a picnic on the banks of the Saône or Rhône.

Travel advice: If you're coming to Lyon via the neighboring Part-Dieu railway station, the market is a fantastic place to start.

9. Wander Down the Saône Riverbank Promenade

The banks of the Saône River are exquisite, providing lovely views of Vieux Lyon and a 9-mile route (or "promenade" that leads you from the city center to the border of the Rhône Valley region.

Explore the riverfront pathways, promenade, and fine footbridges before or after touring Vieux Lyon (passerelles in French). Enjoy the play of light on the river and the warm, magnificent façades of Old Town, particularly at night or in the morning. One of the city's best locations for photos, so makes sure your camera or phone has enough juice.

10. Stop by City Hall (Hôtel de Ville) and Place des Terreaux

1 Pl. de la Comédie, 69001 Lyon, France
PHONE *+33 4 72 10 30 30*

The Place des Terreaux, which is dominated by Lyon's Hôtel de Ville (City Hall), serves as the main thoroughfare for the Presqu'île neighborhood.

The expansive, open center plaza is often utilized for civic events and official processions. It was constructed in a great neoclassical design to replace an older plan destroyed during the French Revolution of 1789. See the striking Bartholdi Fountain, which has a colossal sculpture of a lady in charge of a chariot crossing four French rivers. In 1889, it was finished.

The imposing City Hall of Lyon dominates the east side of the plaza, while the opulent Saint-Pierre Palace is located close to the Lyon Fine Arts Museum at the southern end.

11. Explore the Presqu'île District

Pl. Bellecour, 69002 Lyon, France

PHONE +33 4 72 77 69 69

The bustling center of modern Lyon is this central district between the Rhône and the Saône, which is home to crowded commercial streets, museums, large squares, restaurants, and theaters.

It's design and architecture combine elements of the Renaissance and the 19th century, and many of the area's exquisite facades are reminiscent of Paris' Haussmannian style.

From the Place Bellecour, one of the biggest pedestrian plazas in Europe, to the Place des Terreaux, the Presqu'île extends. A closer location to the banks of the Rhône is where you'll discover the Lyon Opera House, which has a contemporary domed rooftop designed by French architect Jean Nouvel. The Rue Mercière is home to several beautiful Renaissance-era structures.

12. Museum of Fine Arts (Musée des Beaux-Arts) to see famous masterpieces

20 Pl. des Terreaux, 69001 Lyon, France

PHONE +33 4 72 10 17 40

This neighborhood museum on Place des Terreaux is a must-see for anybody with interest in fine art. One of

Europe's biggest and most significant permanent collections, it includes artwork, sculptures, pottery, and artifacts dating from ancient Egypt to the current age.

There are works of art by artists like Véronèse, Rubens, Géricault, Delacroix, Manet, Monet, Gauguin, Picasso, and Matisse, as well as urns, sarcophagi, and everyday items from ancient Egypt that may be admired.

The museum is situated in a remarkable Benedictine monastery from the 17th century. In the late 1990s, it underwent restoration.

13. Unwind in Parc de la Tête d'Or

69006 Lyon, France

PHONE +33 4 72 69 47 60

One of Lyon's most beautiful and sizable municipal parks is the perfect place to get some fresh air or set up a French-style picnic on the grass. The romantic-style Park de la Tête d'Or, which first opened its gates in 1857, beckons tourists through its golden gates to explore its lush walkways, man-made lakes, footbridges, bicycle lanes, and even a small zoo.

After strolling along the Rhône river's banks, visit the park. Children will enjoy activities like mini-golf, pony and horseback riding, puppet shows, and riding the park's own miniature train if you're traveling with them.

14. Go on a wine tour and try some regional wines.

Lyon is located in the lush Rhône Valley, which is home to some of France's greatest wineries and vineyards. We suggest taking a day excursion that includes wine tasting and guided tours of one or more nearby vineyards if you have more than a few days to explore the city.

You may learn about the many terroirs—specific geographic regions known to create quite diverse kinds of wines owing to soil quality, sunshine, etc.—of the Rhône Valley on one of these guided wine excursions. Also, you'll get knowledge on how to appreciate and identify certain notes and tastes in reds and whites. You'll also visit nearby wine-producing facilities to obtain a deeper understanding of the art of winemaking.

15. Museum of Miniatures & Cinema

60 Rue Saint-Jean, 69005 Lyon, France

Fan of the history of film? What about scale models? Both are highlighted in this fascinating double anthology.

The eccentric museum is home to more than 100 beautifully made tiny scenarios of places, including restaurants, movie theaters, apothecaries, old-fashioned doctors' offices, and more.

The cinema collection, meanwhile, has a special effects gallery, images, memorabilia, reproductions of movie sets, costumes, and more. Also, it presents unique, transient exhibitions on many topics, including specific film directors, genres, and themes.

The location in Old Lyon is particularly noteworthy for the structure it is housed in the Maison des Avocats2, a Renaissance masterpiece from the 16th century that is now a UNESCO monument.

16. Marvel at one of Europe's Largest Pieces of Public Art

La Croix-Rousse, 69004 Lyon, France

The Croix-Rousse area is often disregarded by visitors, but it shouldn't be. The Croix-Rousse is Lyon's second largest hill, after Fourvière, and is located at its high heights. It is dotted with trendy shops and eateries, winding walks, and enigmatic courtyards.

Croix-Rousse, the former residence of the canuts, a sizable neighborhood of Lyon's 19th-century silk workers and weavers, still displays signs of that intriguing past. It has several traboules, or tunnels, worth visiting, much like Old Lyon. Local artisans often used them to carry silk.

The Mur des Canuts should not be missed; it is a large "trompe l'oeil" mural that meticulously captures everyday life in the area in the nineteenth century. One of the biggest works of public art in all of Europe.

17. Dig Into the History of Lyon's Silk Workers
10 Rue d'Ivry, 69004 Lyon, France
PHONE +33 4 78 28 62 04
Visit the Maison des Canuts (Silk Workers' Museum) in the center of the Croix-Rousse neighborhood if you want to learn more about the history of Lyon's canuts (silk workers).
You'll get knowledge about the actual technique of silk weaving in addition to everyday living, social circumstances, and well-known revolts of the cants. When you visit the workshop here, you may learn a lot of fascinating facts about anything from the life cycles of silkworms to the labor-intensive and sophisticated process of weaving silk to the development of the Jacquard loom.

18. Honor the Memory of French Jews at the Resistance and Deportation History Center
14 Av. Berthelot, 69007 Lyon, France
PHONE +33 4 72 73 99 00

This significant collection of artifacts and records about the city during World War II, when France's collaborationist government in Vichy, France, engaged in Nazi crimes, brings Lyon's darker past to life.

The documentation center is symbolically placed in Lyon's old Gestapo headquarters, where countless resistance members were tortured. Klaus Barbie, a member of the SS and the head of the Gestapo in Lyon, had his offices here as well. He oversaw the transfer of 7,500 local French Jews to death and detention camps across Europe. Also, he was directly responsible for the deaths of 4,000 people, largely political dissidents.

Visitors may keep alive the memories of the hundreds who died at the hands of both the Nazis and Vichy France by visiting the multimedia display, which is both instructive and enlightening.

19. See How Lyon Became a Powerhouse in the Silk Trade
34 Rue de la Charité, 69002 Lyon, France
PHONE +33 7 63 30 07 43
Visitors may go through 2,000 years of textile history at the Textile & Decorative Arts Museum, which also provides information on the social and economic changes that have surrounded it.

The collection, which includes items like priceless Persian carpets, elaborate tapestries, and silks from all across Europe, recounts the tale of how Lyon emerged as a global leader in the silk trade throughout the Renaissance.

Together with an amazing collection of ancient clocks, it also has a sizeable collection of tapestries from the Renaissance and medieval periods. There is also a current collection of ornamental pieces that demonstrate how preferences and materials changed from the time of the Industrial Revolution to the present.

20. Learn About Some of Lyon's Most Famous Residents: The Lumière Brothers

25 Rue du Premier Film, 69008 Lyon, France

PHONE +33 4 78 78 18 95

You shouldn't be shocked to find that Lyon has two museums devoted to the history of film. The renowned Lumière brothers, natives of Lyon, are credited with creating the first (short) moving pictures. They were innovators in filmmaking methods and technology. The city is pleased with its contributions to the development of the "seventh art" as a result.

Even though Lumière Villa is off the usual road, the beautiful 19th-century structure and its surrounding gardens are worth the trip. You'll discover an amazing collection of objects within that are connected to the filmmaking innovations of the Lumière brothers as well as the history of movies in general.

CHAPTER 9: LYON'S TOP BARS, CLUBS, & OTHER NIGHTLIFE SPOTS

Lyon, one of the biggest towns in France, is known for its rich history and culture as well as its relaxed, interesting, and sophisticated nightlife scene. While the historic Gallo-Roman capital has a reputation for being rather staid and traditional, it has evolved into a more open and lively city in the twenty-first century, which is reflected in the present nightlife scene. There is something for everyone in Lyon, whether your idea of the ideal night out is drinking beautifully crafted cocktails on a river boat, tasting fine wines with cheese and charcuterie platters in a hidden cellar, or dancing till the early hours of the morning in one of the greatest clubs in town. Read on for our advice on where to go, what to do, and how to make the most of your night out.

A wide range of bars can be found in Lyon, ranging from little neighborhood watering holes selling a limited selection of wines and beers to upscale cocktail lounges mixing up inventive concoctions and péniches (boat bars) anchored on the river. On major squares like the Place des Terreaux, where residents often meet for pre-dinner drinks, it's usual to see crowded tables spilling out from popular pubs during the warmer months (aperitifs). Yet during the winter months, sipping wine in a small, dimly lit basement may be relaxing and enjoyable.

The bar scene in Lyon has grown over the last several decades to include more creative, up-to-date nightlife establishments. Do you like a restaurant with a speakeasy-style bar concealed behind a locked door? What about a drink at a rooftop bar where renowned DJs provide the perfect ambiance? The city has undoubtedly moved beyond its previous image as a stuffy financial and commercial center.

We only suggest the following spots for a drink, either before or after dinner:

• The Monkey Club: This upscale cocktail lounge, which is situated atop Place des Terreaux, bills itself as a cross between a Victorian boudoir and a curiosity cabinet. The beverages are both interesting and eye-catching.

• Les Valseuses: This neighborhood pub is rough, cozy, and well-liked by locals. It's one of the finest places in the artistic Croix-Rousse area for a drink and a little meal. It is renowned in particular for its rum variety. Here, live music performances and DJ sets are frequent occurrences.

• Bistrot Têtedoie: Situated high on Fourvière hill, this restaurant and bar provide some of the greatest city views as well as a wide selection of cocktails on its expansive panoramic terrace.

• Le Bootlegger: With its broad leather sofas, wine barrels for tables, and low lighting, this speakeasy-style establishment in the upper sections of Vieux Lyon exudes a "Prohibition era-chic" ambiance. Pure rock makes up the soundtrack.

Nightclubs

Historically, Lyon's nightlife hasn't been very noteworthy, but in recent years, a new generation of local club owners and DJs has altered all that. The variety, eclecticism, and inspiration of clubs in the city are growing. They range from massive clubs situated in abandoned factories to gritty, subterranean basements where experimental jazz and hip-hop concerts are followed by somber techno. With the exception of more upscale locations, cover prices are often acceptable.

• Le Sucre: Located next to the modern Confluences sector and constructed in a former sugar mill, Le Sucre is one of the most cutting-edge locations for a night of dancing to worldwide DJ sets (mostly electro). The rooftop terrace bar offers fantastic cocktails and views.

• La Maison: La Maison offers all you need if you're searching for a more relaxed club atmosphere where you can sip chic drinks. House, disco, and funk dominate themed events and DJ sets. Before the dancing celebration, have a sit-down meal at the restaurant next door.

• Le Petit Salon is one of the hippest places in town for drinking and dancing to daring sets by a rotating cast of DJs. It is located in Lyon's University quarter. Every weekend, hundreds of residents attend concerts in the genres of techno, rap, house, trance, and funk.

• The United Café (UC): Lyon's oldest LGBT-welcoming nightclub, the UC presents drag and karaoke performances in addition to energetic electro events on its large dance floors.

Live musical performance

No matter what kind of music you're in the mood for—jazz, opera, rock, dance-til-you-drop electro—you can easily enjoy an evening of live music in Lyon. The city hosts concerts all year long in a variety of locations, including opulent amphitheaters and riverboats. Some are also cost-effective, with entrance fees that are as low as a tiny cover charge or none at all.

• Le Transbordeur: This venerable musical venue, one of the trendiest in the city, often hosts live performances by artists from across the world. The program includes rock, hip-hop, electronic music, and independent music.

• Le Sirius: This péniche, a boat bar and café anchored on the Rhône is one of Lyon's most well-known. It often has live music performances, ranging from jazz and hip-hop to swing. If you can travel between late spring through early autumn.

• The Periscope: Jazz fans go to this experimental performance café on a regular basis to see performances by national and international artists. There is a bohemian and artistic atmosphere.

• Lyon Opera: Take in a performance of opera or classical music at this striking city landmark, which has a striking domed rooftop constructed by architect Jean Nouvel.

Late-Night Restaurants

Despite being the center of the world's cuisine, Lyon isn't particularly famous for its late-night eating establishments. Even so, you can generally find something to eat these days as you go from club to club late into the evening.

Here are a few we particularly suggest:

• Mama Shelter Lyon: One of Lyon's most well-liked late-night eating establishments, with its vibrantly colored and graffitied walls, tiny but lovely rooftop bar area, and kitchen offering meals till midnight. Some of the most frequent inquiries from our clients are as follows. Thursday through Sunday also includes DJ performances.

• La Gratinée: This steakhouse is open until 7 a.m. and is close to the Fine Arts Museum and Place des Terreaux. It's a great place to eat all night. The menu includes dishes including steak and fries, potatoes au gratin, and another traditional French fare. There are several spaghetti and salad options for vegetarians.

• Le P'tit Cass de Nuit: This snack bar on the Saône river's banks is a favored place to get good tacos and other post-club food since it's open until 3:30 a.m. (closed on Mondays). While you're exploring Vieux Lyon or the center "Presqu'Île" region, it's a nice place to stop.

Festivals

Lyon is a terrific destination to experience after-dark festivals and activities, especially in the late spring through early fall. Be sure to attend open-air performances of music or drama held in the city's historic Gallo-Roman arenas during the yearly Les Nuits de Fourvière. Popular summertime activities like the Eté en Cinemascope festival, which has hundreds of free outdoor film screenings, also take place during this season. For one day only, on June 21, Lyon celebrates music with free concerts all across the city during the Fête de la Musique (and around France).

The harvest festivities for the Beaujolais Nouveau wine (which typically begin in the third week of November) and the Lyon Beer Festival keep the festive spirit alive if you're coming in the autumn.

Tips for Going Out in Lyon

• The major bus lines in Lyon operate until around 10:30 p.m., while the metro and tram lines stay open until 12 or 12:30 a.m. seven days a week (with earlier service end times on Sundays and public holidays). Using the night bus is a possibility beyond these hours, albeit it might be difficult for tourists to utilize. We advise booking a hotel near to the town center so you can quickly stroll there or, in an emergency, take a quick taxi journey.

• If you miss the final bus or metro, you can always grab a cab, and Uber is available in Lyon. Place Bellecour, Hôtel de Ville/Place des Terreaux, and Vieux Lyon are all centrally located areas with taxi stands (Old Lyon). Taxis are often quite busy around 2 a.m. when bars shut.

• Although most nightclubs have separate permits allowing them to stay up until early morning, bars and cafés that serve alcohol are often allowed to stay open until 2 a.m.

• Tipping bartenders is not customarily anticipated in France. Nonetheless, as a modest token of appreciation for the superior service, you may always round up your bill to the next Euro. If you get service at a table, it is usual to leave a tip of between five and ten percent of the entire amount charged.

• The nighttime temperatures in late autumn and winter may be brisk, with temperatures sometimes falling below freezing in January and February. On your night out during the cooler months, particularly if it involves walking about, be sure to wear or carry along a heavy coat, gloves, scarf, and warm socks.

CHAPTER 10: THE 10 BEST HOTELS IN LYON

A key part of the planning process for anybody organizing a trip to Lyon is selecting the ideal lodging. The former Gallo-Roman capital, one of France's most significant towns, has a large number of hotels, but how do you choose the best one for you? For a list of the top hotels in Lyon, with options for every price range and style, continue reading. The choices below should have something to suit your requirements, whether you're looking for a luxury hotel with stunning city views or a cozy, no-frills budget alternative.

1. Villa Florentine

25 Mnt Saint-Barthélémy, 69005 Lyon, France

PHONE +33 4 72 56 56 56

The five-star Villa Florentine, located in the center of Old Lyon and near the Saône riverfront region, has consistently garnered accolades for its large rooms, opulent facilities, scenic location, and first-rate service. It belongs to the exclusive Relais et Chateaux hotel chain.

The hotel's 29 air-conditioned rooms and suites, which are housed in a former convent, are furnished in French and Florentine styles and come with king-sized mattresses with luxurious linens, a bathtub, an LED TV, upscale amenities, and a welcome tray with tea, espresso, and bottled water. A breathtaking view of the Gothic Saint-Jean Cathedral, the roofs of Old Lyon, and beyond may be enjoyed from the spacious heated outdoor pool and deck area. There's also an onsite spa and gourmet restaurant.

The current nightly fee for this hotel is between $240 and $280; Villa Florentine assures the lowest prices when making a reservation on its own website.

2. Hotel de l'Abbaye

20 Rue de l'Abbaye d'Ainay, 69002 Lyon, France

PHONE +33 4 78 05 60 40

In Lyon's downtown Ainay neighborhood, this 4-star boutique hotel strikes a seductive mix between classic old-world charm and cutting-edge modernity. The independent hotel, which is located on a peaceful plaza not far from the Basilica of St. Martin d'Ainay church, is renowned for its top-notch personnel and tourist services, elegant and comfortable accommodations, and affordability.

There is complimentary Wi-Fi, air conditioning, blackout curtains, plush bedding, a coffee and tea maker, a desk, and flatscreen TVs with international cable channels in the tastefully appointed rooms and suites, which are all themed in various themes. Some accommodations provide magnificent city views. The onsite restaurant, l'Artichaut, offers a wide selection of wines together with contemporary French cuisine. The lunch and supper set-price meals are substantial and affordable.

Currently, this hotel's nightly rates vary from around $215 to $290.

3. The Celestins Hotel

4 Rue des Archers, 69002 Lyon, France

PHONE +33 4 72 56 08 98

Between the huge Place de Bellecour plaza and the Place des Jacobins, this privately owned 3-star hotel is situated in the heart of the city. It has received praise for its cozy but rustic accommodations, welcoming staff, convenient location, and overall value for money.

The hotel's air-conditioned rooms are furnished in a typical French manner, and they have a homey feel that can make you think of a B&B. Free Wi-Fi, free coffee, amenities, a safe, a hairdryer, and a flatscreen TV with international cable channels are all included in the rooms. Some rooms provide views of the city or the courtyard; if you want sweeping vistas, consider staying in the rooftop suite. There is a breakfast buffet. The employees are multilingual, including in English.

The current nightly prices at this hotel vary from around $120 to $135.

4. Fourvière Hotel

23 Rue Roger Radisson, 69005 Lyon, France

PHONE +33 4 74 70 07 00

This beautiful 4-star hotel, housed in a historic convent atop Fourvière hill, is a great option for couples or vacationers looking for a unique but opulent environment. The hotel has two restaurants, a spa, and an outdoor heated pool and is only steps from the Fourvière basilica, the Gallo-Roman museum, and theaters. It includes a 24-hour reception and is accessible to guests in wheelchairs and with restricted mobility.

Three stories house the 75 rooms and suites (try to get a top-floor room for the best views over the city rooftops and basilica). All rooms are equipped with free Wi-Fi, air conditioning, a minibar, a safe, and free access to the pool and spa. They are all decorated in a simple, modern design with wood flooring and brightly colored furniture.

Now, prices per night vary from around $155 to $400.

5. Hotel Vaubecour

28 Rue Vaubecour 2é étage, 69002 Lyon, France

PHONE +33 4 78 37 44 91

The 2-star Hotel Vaubecour, which has received high marks for cleanliness, comfy mattresses, a great breakfast, pleasant service, and value for money, maybe the ideal option for tourists on a tight budget. The Saône riverbanks and Old Lyon are just a short stroll away from this central Lyon location, which is situated between the Place Bellecour and Perrache station.

The hotel's 15 rooms, which are housed in a 19th-century structure, are designed in a modern manner with vintage accents like antique mirrors and ceiling moldings. Smart Televisions, free Wi-Fi, a welcome tray with tea and coffee, a baggage rack, and a hairdryer are included in every room. Convertible sofas and small fridges are available in junior suites. The hotel has a breakfast area where guests may enjoy continental breakfast items, including freshly baked bread and pastries from nearby bakeries.

Now, nights cost an average of $95 to $150.

6. Cours des Loges

6 Rue du Boeuf, 69005 Lyon, France

PHONE +33 4 72 77 44 44

This five-star hotel is tucked away in Vieux Lyon and is known for its lovely and historic location. Its grounds include exquisite Renaissance-era traboules (arched passageways).

The Cours des Loges, which has a heated indoor pool, spa, and Michelin-starred restaurant called Les Loges, cultivates an antique look that combines French and Italian inspirations. Luxury bedding, painted walls, and furnishings, a minibar, a refrigerator, a flatscreen TV with free entertainment, a safe, and room service are all included in the opulently designed, air-conditioned rooms and suites. The current nightly prices for this place vary from around $190 to $315. Direct reservations made through the official website provide the lowest prices.

7. Hotel des Savoies Lyon-Perrache

80 Rue de la Charité, 69002 Lyon, France

PHONE +33 4 78 37 66 94

The Hotel des Savoies, which is conveniently adjacent to the Perrache railway station, is another excellent midrange lodging choice in Lyon. Travelers endorse the hotel for its reliable comforts, cleanliness, and affordability while also providing easy access to the city center, TGV rail station, and airport.

The 44 rooms on the property are furnished with double beds, air conditioning, Wi-Fi, flatscreen TVs with international cable channels, safes, and courtesy trays. They are all styled in a modern manner. You may get a free copy of the book from the library or get it online.

Currently, nights at this hotel cost between $90 and $105 per person. By making a direct reservation on the official website, the best pricing is guaranteed.

8. Mama Shelter Lyon

13 Rue Domer, Lyon, France 69007

PHONE +33 4 78 02 58 00

This 2-star hotel is a member of the Mama Shelter chain of hotels, which is renowned for providing inexpensive lodging with onsite entertainment, restaurants, and a cool modern ambiance. It is located in Lyon's artistic 7th arrondissement. The hotel has a sizable bar, restaurant, and expansive patio that are great for drinks, games of foosball, and live DJ sets, making it a great choice for youthful tourists and night owls.

Thankfully, the 156 rooms in the hotel are described as soundproof (though some travelers report otherwise). Free

Wi-Fi, air conditioning, plush bedding, organic in-room products, a safe, and a smart TV with free movies and other entertainment choices are all included in standard rooms. Now, nights cost between $140 and $190.

9. Intercontinental Hotel-Dieu

20 Quai Jules Courmont, 69002 Lyon, France

PHONE +33 4 26 99 23 23

Another great option for a luxurious, romantic stay in Lyon is this 5-star Intercontinental hotel, which is just a few steps from the lively Place Bellecour and the banks of the Rhône river. The hotel is housed in a beautiful 18th-century structure with views of the river and provides rooms that are roomy, light, and airy with modern design features.

Air conditioning, Wi-Fi, a minibar, a safe, a desk, blackout curtains, extra-long mattresses with luxurious linens, and room service are amenities offered in the rooms and suites. Full baths are standard in superior rooms and suites, and some have views of the city or river. The hotel also has a gourmet French restaurant, a complete bar, a fitness center, a sauna, a 24-hour front desk, and a relaxing terrace in the backyard.

The current advertised nightly prices are between $345 and $430.

10. Ibis Budget Lyon Centre-Part Dieu

52 Rue de la Villette, Lyon, France, 69003; 3E Arr

PHONE +33 892 70 12 75

Here we've compiled answers to some of the most frequently asked questions our clients have concerning our offerings. The hotel provides easy access to the Lyon Part-Dieu rail and metro station as well as the Lyon-Saint Exupéry Airport by nearby TGV (high-speed rail) trains. The historic city center may be reached easily by metro or by walking.

The contemporary rooms at this hotel have typically received positive reviews from guests for comfort and functionality. Free Wi-Fi, a flatscreen TV with international cable channels, air conditioning, a tea and coffee maker, bath amenities, and room service choices are all included in every room. The hotel provides complimentary continental breakfasts and airport transportation. Visitors in wheelchairs and others with limited mobility may also access it.

The current nightly rates for this hotel vary from around $60 to $100.

CHAPTER 11: WHEN TO VISIT LYON: THE IDEAL MOMENT

Lyon, one of the most significant cities in France, is renowned for its architecture, history, cuisine, and museums. Moreover, it serves as a handy entryway to the French south and the Alps. So when is the ideal season to go to the ancient Gallo-Roman city? The finest season to visit Lyon, in the opinion of the majority, is from late spring to mid-autumn when events like outdoor dining, winery tours, and a variety of festivals are at their most popular.

But the end of the year is also a great time to visit since the city comes to life with Christmas lights and celebrations. Find out which season could be ideal for you by reading on.

The Weather in Lyon

Due to its generally high average temperatures, Lyon has a humid subtropical climate that almost seems oceanic. In contrast to winters, which are often cold and dry, summers are frequently hot with frequent storms and heat waves. Summertime temperatures average about 81 F (27 C) for highs and 61 F for lows (16 C). While warmer than in other French locations, the winters may nevertheless bring temperatures that are close to or even just below freezing. Wintertime highs are typically about 44 F (6.5 C), and chilly 34 F lows (1 C).

With increasingly warm and bright circumstances beginning in May, spring is typically warm.

Peak Season in Lyon

In Lyon, the months of late spring through early October are the tourist season. Although summer is famous for outdoor concerts and festivals, the late spring delivers longer, often bright days excellent for outdoor dinners, sightseeing, and day outings. Nonetheless, autumn is the best time of year for wine sampling at local vineyards. Flights and hotel rooms tend to be more costly during the summer and other high travel months. Be sure to make your travel arrangements well in advance if you want to go to France during these busy months.

Traveling in Off-Season

Off-season travel to Lyon (approximately November to early April) has several advantages, including calmer surroundings and fewer people; cheaper flight, train tickets, and accommodation prices; and a chance to see the city from a more local perspective. Going off-season, however, may also have some serious drawbacks, such as shorter days and sometimes colder weather, fewer tour options, and a city that's typically a little less welcoming to visitors. Be sure the sites, eateries, and guided tours you're interested in will be open or operational if you do decide to go during the off-season.

Spring

Although Lyon's spring isn't as overrun with visitors as Paris' is, it still has many of the same allure: beautiful blossoms and greenery; milder temperatures perfect for strolls, picnics, and day excursions; farmers' markets brimming with fresh vegetables; and longer days. Enjoy leisurely strolls along the Rhône and Saône rivers while also visiting Lyon's Botanical Gardens to take in the springtime blooms. See the nicest brocantes (antique markets) in Lyon while sipping coffee on a patio with views of Place des Terreaux.

Check-out Event:

• The Le Printemps des Docks trade exhibition showcases artisanal cuisine, apparel, jewelry, home goods, and more. It is a current design event.

Summer

In the summer, Lyon can be quite picturesque, particularly in the evening when the lit bridges, riverside quays, and meandering lanes truly come to life. Set up a picnic in a park or along the Saône, and then go to the observation platform outside Fourvière Basilica for breathtaking views of the city at sunset. Take in live music, eat outside on city patios, and participate in summer street celebrations like Lyon Pride. In the summer, the long days and nights appear to go on forever.

Events to Check Out:

• During a long night of festivities on June 21, the Fête de la Musique brings free musical performances to Lyon's streets.

• Lyon Pride (Fierté) is a week-long celebration that takes place in June; it is the second-largest gay pride event in France and features street parties and a parade (Marche des Fiertés).

• Live performances of music, drama, and dance are presented during the Nuits de Fourvière event in the city's Roman amphitheaters in late June and early July.

Fall

Lyon's autumn is crisp and motivational. By late October, the summer throngs have really started to drop out, and a warm but energetic atmosphere has taken hold. The air becomes colder, and the temperatures decrease, yet bright days are still frequent. Reserve a table on a spectacular rooftop terrace, wander around the city's most intriguing districts, take a guided tour of local vineyards and wineries, and enjoy the stunning autumn leaves at the lovely Park de la Tete d'Or.

Event to Check Out:
• During the third week of November, the region's vineyards and wine bars host special tasting events to commemorate the Beaujolais Nouveau wines.

Winter

A journey to Lyon in the winter may be enjoyable and restful. Take in a filling lunch in one of the city's cozy, traditional bouchons before exploring the booths at the renowned covered market, Les Halles Paul Bocuse. Take advantage of warm seasonal activities like winter lights and markets by dressing warmly and strolling around Old Lyon. The city's several fascinating museums provide a fun way to stay warm. Lastly, for a winter escape straight out of a storybook, think about taking a day trip to one of the neighboring Alpine villages, like Annecy.

Grammarly from here downward with plagiarism checker

Events to Check Out:

• Beginning in late November, the city's largest Christmas market (Marché de Nol) takes over the sizable Place Carnot plaza in the heart of the city, with over 140 kiosks selling festive merchandise including toys, decorations, mulled wine, and crêpes.

• On December 8, take in the Fête des Lumières (Festival of Lights), a Lyonnais celebration in which several buildings across the city are transformed into glowing spectacles. Votive candles are also often placed in windows by locals, creating a captivating and unforgettable impression.

Chapter 12: Restaurants in Lyon: The Top 11

Being the culinary capital of France, Lyon is home to an astounding array of top-notch eateries, from cozy bouchons (the city's customary, family-owned tables) to classic bistros, Michelin-starred locations, and informal brasseries. Read on for our recommendations for some of Lyon's top eateries, with an emphasis on more conventional, classic settings and a few cutting-edge newbies.

1. La Mère Brazier

12 Rue Royale, Lyon, France 69001

PHONE +33 4 78 23 17 20

This upscale restaurant, which Eugénie Brazier first opened in 1921, is the stuff of neighborhood lore. Brazier was the first woman in France to get three Michelin stars and one of the renowned Mères Lyonnaises, female restaurant owners who began their careers as domestic chefs for aristocratic households.

The renowned table is now run by celebrity chef Mathieu Vianny, who has successfully ushered it into a modern new era while retaining significant parts from Madame Brazier's hallmark dishes. While not cheap, the menus at this two-star Michelin restaurant are affordable given the quality. Enjoy a starter of wild mushroom fricassee or sea bream marinated with black garlic and plums before moving on to glazed pigeon with colorful beets and kumquats with pepper for the main meal. Ask your waitress for advice on wine pairings for the various meals. The cheese plates include seasonal options from regional suppliers.

The greatest value may be found on lunch menus, which are available every day except Saturday.

2. Daniel et Denise

Daniel & Denise, regarded as one of the best bouchons in the city, is owned and operated by Joseph Viola, a renowned chef who won the famous meilleur ouvrier de France award for his inventive food combined with French heritage. With red-and-white gingham tablecloths and tiled flooring, the little eating area is conventional and simple. Start with a silky soup like pumpkin velouté, then go on to whole Bresse chicken with morel mushrooms or pike quenelles, which are fish dumplings with crayfish flavoring. Also well-known are Viola's meat pies (pâté en croute). If you are on a limited budget but yet want to pamper yourself while traveling, the fixed-price meals are an excellent option, especially for lunch.

Daniel et Denise runs eateries in Old Lyon, the steep Croix-Rousse neighborhood, and the surrounding town of Villeurbanne, in addition to their primary outlet at the Halles de Lyon market.

3. Le Nord

18 Rue Neuve, Lyon, France 69002

PHONE +33 4 72 10 69 69

Le Nord is one of four geographically named brasseries in Lyon that the renowned chef Paul Bocuse built. It has marble flooring, vintage globe lighting, a large copper bar, and tables covered in white tablecloths.

This centrally located table is just to the south of the Hôtel de Ville (City Hall). Here, the emphasis is on using market-fresh products, and the three- and four-course Lyonnais menus provide good value. Enjoy the restaurant's take on French onion soup, hoarding-sauteed pike quenelle, traditional Lyonnais salad, roast chicken, or saucisson in a pistachio-crusted shell. The wine selection is limited but full of great options, and the cheeses and sweets are plentiful and fantastic. A fresh, spreadable Lyonnais cheese prepared with fromage blanc, herbs, and spices is called cervelle de canut; be sure to sample it. Moreover, the praline tart is said to be outstanding.

4. Brasserie Georges

Lyon, France (69022) 30 Cr de Verdun Perrache

PHONE +33 4 72 56 54 54

This vast, always busy restaurant in Lyon first opened its doors in 1836 and is still highly sought after by foodies today. Brasserie Georges is a popular eatery with red leather seats, elaborate murals, and enormous mirrors that help to create an old-world atmosphere that makes even a regular lunch seem extraordinary. It is conveniently situated close to Place Carnot and the Gare de Perrache railway station. While being famous for its sauerkraut, the restaurant serves all of the traditional French brasserie fare, including fish and chips, sausages cooked in wine, and crispy chocolate and praline cake. There are also a few good vegetarian alternatives available here. There is also a nice assortment of craft beers from the on-site brewery on the beer menu, which is noteworthy. For smaller budgets, daily specials and fixed-price lunch menus are appropriate.

5. La Bouchon Sully

20 Rue Sully, Lyon, France 69006

PHONE +33 4 78 89 07 09

This relatively recent addition to the Lyonnais bouchon scene is located on the east bank of the Rhône, right next to Parc de la Tête d'Or, and it has just been included in the Michelin Guide for its basic yet excellent cuisine. Le Bouchon Sully, run by Julien Gautier, who is also the proprietor of the adjacent M Restaurant, provides a carefully crafted menu of time-honored favorites with a dash of modern flair. Begin with the beet salad that comes with pine nuts, a soft-boiled egg, and horseradish emulsion before moving on to the vol au vent that comes with sweetbreads, chicken quenelles, prawns, mushrooms, and "supreme" sauce for your main meal. Instead, choose the veal liver served with potatoes and sautéed with fresh parsley. For dessert, try the soufflé with chartreuse liqueur and red wine-poached pear or a cheese board piled high with creamy regional specialties. The restaurant offers an exceptional range of French wines, primarily from the nearby areas, on its comprehensive wine list.

6. Culina Hortus

Address: 38 Rue de l'Arbre Sec, Lyon, France, 69001

PHONE +33 4 69 84 71 08

This table, which is one of the few vegetarian establishments in Lyon to get excellent gourmet reviews, was established in 2016 by Thomas Bouanich and Maxime Rémond and is located just across the street from their other eatery Victoire & Thomas. There are no dull lentil casseroles or squishy fake meat dishes at Culina Hortus, which is run by chef Adrien Zedda and concentrates on integrating vegetables and plants in culinary innovation.

Instead, you can anticipate exquisitely designed, intelligent dishes made of seasonal ingredients; vibrant tastes and unexpected connections keep things exciting. The use of premium, specially obtained ingredients—from Bordier butter to regional wild herbs—is strongly emphasized. The tasting menus provide a real culinary experience since they are built around various themes, textures, and ingredients. The items on the tasting menus are best paired with a carefully curated choice of natural and biodynamic wines.

7. Brasserie de l'Ouest

One Quai du Commerce, Lyon, France, 69009

PHONE +33 4 37 64 64 64

Brasserie de l'Ouest is the perfect choice for superb Lyonnais food in a more modern atmosphere. A member of the Bocuse Brasserie group, this utterly contemporary, open-plan restaurant has a large eating area with a glass wall showcasing a substantial selection of regional, French, and foreign wines. Locals like Brasserie de l'Ouest's fixed-price Sunday menu, which includes an appetizer, a main course, and a dessert. French classics are given fusion-inspired seasonal twists by chef Charlie Dumas, who also prepares dishes like sea bass with wild mushrooms, Bigorre pig with vegetables and fall fruits, and French veal with potatoes and white onions. Try the Valhrona chocolate tart or the house-made Paris Brest (chou pastry with hazelnut biscuit, coffee cream, and custard). Get wine recommendations from your server for one or more of your courses. If it's warm outside, take a seat on the expansive terrace that looks out over the Saône river.

8. Le Café des Federations

9 Rue Major Martin, 69001 Lyon, France

PHONE +33 4 78 28 26 00

Have a full stomach and go over to this lovely, well-deservedly well-liked Lyon Bouchon. In the Plaza des Terreaux on the "island" in the middle of the city lies Le Café de la Fédération, a vibrant and popular restaurant with tiled floors, rustic wooden tables, and red gingham tablecloths. Both the décor and the cuisine are quite traditional, and both are really good. The traditional menu gives diners a choice between four daily starters, including herring rillette, Lyonnais salad, and local charcuterie. Other hot main course choices include boudin noir (black pork sausage), veal with morel mushrooms, and chicken in vinegar; the overflowing cheese plates are excellent for dessert or a third meal. Try the pink praline pie, a beloved Lyon classic, for dessert. Splash it all down with a glass of local Beaujolais or Morgan red wine.

9. La Sud

11 Place Antonin Poncet, Lyon, France, 69002

PHONE +33 4 72 77 80 00

Le Sud, another coveted table in the Brasserie Bocuse chain of eateries, is dedicated to the Provençal and Mediterranean gourmet traditions. It has all the charm and viva de vivre of the area it draws its inspiration from and is just a short distance from the busy Place Bellecour in the city center. Olive oil, seasonal fresh vegetables, Provençal herbs, and other sunny ingredients are the star of the show in many of the meals served here. The two-course set menus are a great bargain and include traditional dishes like risottos, pissaladière (a Provençal dish with anchovies and olives), chicken pastilla (paella) with Moroccan spices, fresh fish with vegetables, and tajines in the Moroccan manner. Another suggested dinner is the three-course, dessert-filled Sunday menu. Eat outside on warm days to get the full Mediterranean flavor.

10. Le Bouchon des Cordeliers

15 Rue Claudia, Lyon, France 69002

PHONE +33 4 78 03 33 53

Local favorite Le Bouchon des Cordeliers is located in the city center close to the banks of the Rhône river and is renowned for both its amiable, relaxed service and superb food. The cuisine is overseen by Chef Cédric Garin, who offers a straightforward yet outstanding menu of Lyonnais delicacies built on regional, seasonally appropriate fruits and meats. The fresh fish of the day served with root vegetables and an emulsion of morel mushrooms is one example of a main course; another is pâté en croûte (meat pie) stuffed with three different kinds of poultry, Colonnata bacon, and pickled red onions. Desserts are customary and delectable; among the currently available options is a lemon pie with Italian meringue. Try the three-course Menu des Canuts, which is offered every day, for the greatest value. The wine selection is well-chosen and concentrates on fermented grapes from the regions of Burgundy, Beaujolais, and the Côtes du Rhone.

11. L'Est

14 Place Jules Ferry, Lyon, France 69006

PHONE +33 4 37 24 25 26

This last member of the Bocuse family of Lyonnais brasseries has an emphasis on cuisine from the far east. The dining room, which is situated in the historic neighborhood near the ancient Brotteaux station, has a miniature train that wraps around the ceiling to serve as a reminder of the area's historical past. Clocks on the wall display the time in four different parts of the globe. Despite the modest tables and white tablecloths, the atmosphere here is lovely, and the walls are decorated with old posters. Asian-inspired foods are combined with French brasserie favorites on the lunch and supper menus, which are either à la carte or fixed-price. You may have the king prawns with basil, lemon, and sweet chili sauce; the prawns and squid in Cantonese rice; or the filet of beef with shallots, red cabbage, wild mushrooms, and red wine sauce. A classic rum baba, a "Vacherin" meringue dish with red fruits, and a variety of cheeses are offered as desserts. The Sunday fixed-price meal at the Bocuse brasseries is a fantastic deal.

CHAPTER 13: 10 MUST-EATS WHILE IN LYON

Lyon is largely considered France's gastronomic capital, home to some of the world's top chefs and restaurants. Even if you're not on a Michelin-star restaurant budget (like most of us), you should never pass up the opportunity to sample some of the city's finest traditional meals and delicacies. These are the top ten typical meals to try in Lyon, along with some recommendations on where to eat them. They range from seafood to cheeses, pastries, and desserts.

1. Cervelle de Canut Cheese

The name of this meal may cause those with just rudimentary high school or college French to raise an eyebrow since it may give the impression that "brains" are included. The dish's name, which refers to the canuts who produced and sold silks in Lyon during the 19th century, literally translates to "silk workers' brains," thus, your French studies were successful.

Do not worry, as cervelle de canut is a type of soft cheese that is commonly enjoyed as a spread or dip along with crusty bread. This aromatic dip originated from Lyon and is prepared using ingredients such as shallots, chives, parsley (and/or other herbs), olive oil, salt, pepper, and a small amount of lemon juice or vinegar. The cheese used in making cervelle de canut is fromage blanc, which is a creamy and light cheese that is similar to sour cream.

Where to eat: Most traditional, family-run eateries (bouchons) in the Lyon area serve cervelle de canut. Also, it is generally accessible at markets and cheese stores.

2. Quenelles de Brochet (Pike Dumplings)

This iconic Lyonnais meal is simple yet challenging to execute well. In order to make dumplings (also known as quenelles), delicate pike fish filets are mixed with flour, eggs, milk, cream, butter, and seasonings. The quenelles are then poached and served with a rich sauce, generally "sauce Nantua," which is made of béchamel flavored with crayfish butter.

If fish isn't your thing, quenelles come in a wide range of various flavors, such as nature (plain), quenelles de veau (veal dumplings), and chicken.

Where you may eat: Every traditional Lyon bouchon will have its own take on the city's emblematic dish, but Le Bouchon des Cordeliers and Chez Chabert are renowned for serving particularly mouthwatering versions.

3. Pink Praline Tart

The pink praline pie, a specialty that is as cheery and jovial as it is delicious, is one delicacy that you should not miss when visiting Lyon. This straightforward dessert will appeal to anybody who likes the nutty, crunchy delight of praline candy. Beginning with pink pralines—almonds or hazelnuts coated in sugar and dyed pink to mimic raspberries—a Lyon specialty in and of itself. They are gently cooked in heavy cream before being piled on top of a decadent, almond-infused butter crust. Sometimes crème anglaise or cream is served with it.

Where to sample: This regional delicacy is available at most Lyon bakeries.

4. Lyonnais Sausages

With Lyon's long history with sausages, carnivores among you should have no trouble finding a variety of mouthwatering sausages to sample. The cured pig sausage or salami, known as Rosette de Lyon, is particularly well-liked and easily accessible at boucheries (butcher stores) across the city. It is often flavored with garlic, wine, sea salt, and sometimes other herbs. Crushed black pepper is often used to coat the outside.

Rosette is often served on charcuterie plates with local cheeses, sliced thickly, and paired with a robust glass of red wine. There are also popular beef-based variations for those who don't eat pork.

Where to taste: For some superb Lyonnais sausages, including rosette, visit the Halles Paul Bocuse market.

5. Saint-Marcellin Cheese

This creamy, tasty cheese is a local favorite and is consumed in both formal and casual situations. It hails from the adjacent town of Saint-Marcellin. The semi-soft cheese is often shaped into rounds and made from raw cow's milk that has been gently salted. It has a golden exterior and a creamy, semi-liquid core.

You can purchase the cheese during one of its three ripening stages, which are called sec (dry and the youngest and most solid stage), crémeux (creamy and slightly aged), and bleu (at this point, the cheese has a softer center and a slightly blue hue on the rind). Your choice should depend on your personal preferences.

Try the Arômes de Lyon (flavors of Lyon), Saint-Marcellin cheese that has been aged in white wine. Also, brandy may be used to heal it.

Where to sample: Good examples of this local cheese are available in fromageries (cheese stores) all across the city. A reliable choice is the Halles de Lyon Paul Bocuse market.

6. Pâté en Croute

The pâté-en-croute, or crusted paté, will satisfy your need for pastries and charcuterie. This ancient cuisine, which dates to the Middle Ages, was formerly seen as very boring and out-of-date, but in recent years it has acquired appeal once more. Chefs from all over the globe compete in Lyon in an annual contest to produce inventive iterations of the dish.

Pork is combined with duck foie gras, veal, egg, parsley, garlic, salt, and pepper to make the classic Lyonnais pâté-en-route. Slivers of pistachio are also sometimes included. A buttery shortcrust is then used to carefully enclose the pâte. Typically as a beginning, the meal is commonly served with salad.

The pastry itself was seldom consumed throughout the Middle Ages; instead, it served to preserve the meat. Of course, that's not the case anymore; the greatest dishes in this category have excellent, properly cooked crusts.

Where to eat: Some of the greatest pâté-en-route in town are allegedly served at the legendary Lyonnais bouchon Daniel & Denise. In Lyon, there are several places.

7. Coussin de Lyon (Chocolate)

For those of you with a sweet craving, here is another Lyonnais pleasure you shouldn't miss. Lyon cushions, also known as Coussins de Lyon, are tiny, light-green marzipan candies that are filled with delicately flavored chocolate ganache.

The cousins, which were invented in 1897 by Lyonnais pastry and sweets expert Voisin, are a reference to the silk pillows used in Catholic celebrations honoring the Virgin Mary in the 17th century. The candies may be purchased separately or in tiny bags, but they are often packaged in velvet boxes that resemble couches.

Where to taste: You can get coussins at specialty confectioneries all across Lyon, but you should go right to the source and enjoy them at Voisin.

8. Lyonnaise Salad

Endives and/or other strongly flavored greens, smoked lardons (French-style bacon pieces), a poached or soft-boiled egg, and bread croutons makeup salade lyonnaise. While the straightforward meal is a common main or side at bistro restaurants all year round, it may be a particularly filling choice in the winter when you're not quite hungry enough for some of the city's heavier dishes. Several eateries add seasonal vegetables, red onion, herbs, or cheese to their salads to change it up. Often, a tart Dijon-mustard vinaigrette is served with it.

Where to try: Bouchons and a la carte café-brasseries all throughout Lyon provide this well-liked meal.

9. Tablier de Sapeur (Breaded Beef Tripes)

Even though it's a hallmark of Lyonnais cuisine, this meal is likely only to appeal to brave carnivores. Still, it's worth trying. Beef tripes are used to make the dish tablier de sapeur (sapper's apron), which is then pan-fried after being coated in breadcrumbs and marinated in white wine. The meal is often topped with sauce gribiche, a chives-flavored mayonnaise-like sauce that is frequently served with potatoes or other seasonal vegetables.

Where to eat: Lyon's traditional bouchons often offer their own variations of this well-known meal. In particular, Au Petit Bouchon Chez Georges is well known for it.

10. Bugnes (Lyon-style doughnuts)

Doughnuts are often not associated with French pastry-making, but this Lyon specialty disproves that notion. Bugnes are gently lemon-flavored pastries that are deep-fried before being dusted with powdered sugar. Bugnes, a favorite during Mardi Gras, is sometimes flavored with rum and/or orange blossom extract.

Where to eat: During Mardi Gras, you may get them at several Lyonnais bakeries, and from late January to March, they are often simple to locate. La Marquise Bakery in Old Town is known for its delectable version, while Colibri in Lyon's 6th arrondissement offers a unique dairy-free version for vegans.

CHAPTER 14: THE 6 BEST PARKS IN LYON

Lyon is a relatively green city that is tucked away in the Rhone Valley at the confluence of the Rhone and Saône rivers. The strolls along the river alone may be delightful, plus it is surrounded by vineyards and rolling hills. Even so, you sometimes need a great park to go to for a peaceful walk, a picnic on the grass, or a play date with restless kids. These are the nicest parks in Lyon, ranging from broad, green squares to sizable parks replete with lakes and grottoes, playgrounds, and botanical gardens.

1. Parc de la Tête d'Or

Lyon, France 69006

PHONE +33 4 72 69 47 60

The Park de la Tête d'Or (Parc of the Golden Head), the biggest and most magnificent green area in the heart of Lyon, is a great place for a leisurely walk, a picnic, kid-friendly activities, and (in the fall) leaf-peeping.

This beautiful urban oasis is situated in the elegant 6th arrondissement on the east bank of the Rhone and was established in 1857, the same year Central Park in New York City was established. The almost 300-acre park has a vast Romantic design. Many roomy walkways for walkers and joggers, hundreds of different kinds of trees, flowers, bushes, and plants, as well as manufactured lakes and grottoes where ducks, geese, and other wild birds congregate, are all woven throughout the area. It is highly sought after by locals for its jogging and cycling pathways, spacious picnic areas, and, during the summer, boating on the lake.

Have fun with it: Take a leisurely stroll around the twisting walkways after passing through the great golden gates and seeing the wide varieties of trees, flowers, and plants that line the walks. Stop by the park's several exquisite flowerbeds, and four rose gardens in the spring to see the beauty; in the autumn, the foliage often changes to striking yellows, oranges, and reds. Youngsters will like the mini-golf course, the tiny railway that circles the park, and the zoo, where you can view animals like giraffes, elephants, and monkeys. There is a puppet theater as well. If you still need to bring a picnic, there are various snack bars and more formal eateries in and around the park. By adding a trip to Lyon's Botanical Gardens, whose entrance is at the southernmost point of the Park de la Tête d'Or, you may extend your day.

2. Botanical Gardens at the Tête d'Or

France's Tête d'Or, 69006 Lyon

PHONE +33 4 72 69 47 78

The Lyon Botanical Gardens, which are situated at the southernmost point of the Park de la Tête d'Or, have one of Europe's greatest collections of plant species and hold some 15,000 different types of plants in its greenhouses and carefully maintained outdoor areas. The gardens, which cover around 20 acres, have an international rose garden, a number of greenhouses with specific themes, an orangery, an Alpine garden with about 1,700 alpine plant species indigenous to the Alps, an arboretum, a collection of ferns, and various other places.

Having fun with it: To experience the plants, flowers, and trees at their finest, visit from late April to June. Access the gardens via Avenue Verguin, stroll through the outside areas, and then tour the many greenhouses, taking time to see the excellent architectural aspects and the flora they are home to. The Mexican garden (open from April to October) is worth a visit, and the ancient rose garden displays more than 360 varieties of roses in various dramatic hues. At the Lambert Farm, which has a herbarium with hundreds of thousands of species, a seed shop, a lab for uncommon plants, and a botanical library, visitors of all ages may have an educational experience.

3. Parc des Hauteurs (Heights Park)

Pl. de Fourvière, Lyon, France, 69005

PHONE +33 4 72 69 47 60

The Park des Hauteurs is a green oasis among the heights of the historic city. It is a green belt on Fourvière hill that runs behind the Basilica of the same name. The urban park's winding pathways connect the main Esplanade at Fourviere basilica with the Loyasse cemetery and old fort, a lovely rose garden, and the archeological garden (where you can see artifacts from Lyon's Gallo-Roman period and society). These pathways were built on an abandoned tram track and are known as La Passerelle des Quatre-vents.

Have fun with it: Go along the Quatre-Vents walk after visiting the rose garden at the base of the Basilica for stunning views of the Basilica, beautiful gardens, and historic convent buildings. As you go farther down the hill, the trail will finally lead you to Old Lyon and the banks of the Saône river, providing you with magnificent vistas of the city.

4. Parc Blandan

37 Rue du Repos, Lyon, France, 69007

PHONE +33 4 72 10 30 30

On the site of a former military fort, this intriguing new park was built in 2014. In 2019, it underwent a large expansion that added many acres of green space and recreational amenities. It's positioned at the meeting point of many different Lyon districts, with the entrance in the residential 7th arrondissement.

The Parc Blandan, which consists of three major areas—the fortress, the moats, and a large open area called L'Esplanade—combines historic buildings with cutting-edge urban planning. It is a great place for strolls, picnics, sporting events, and sundowners. A vast "prairie" with lots of green grass for play or leisure, walking trails, and hundreds of kinds of plants and trees make it a green oasis amid an urban setting.

Have fun with it: See the ruins of the old military fort and marvel at its impressive features as you stroll around the park's nearly mile-long perimeter. On one of the picnic tables already set up or on the surrounding grassy "prairie," you may have a picnic. Children will enjoy the spacious playground next to the "Sardou" square, which has toboggans and a climbable wall with hidden pathways.

5. Parc de la Cerisaie

25 Rue Chazière, 69004 Lyon, France

PHONE +33 4 72 69 47 60

You could assume that this park and manor are full of cherry trees from its name, which is "Cherry Tree Park," in direct translation. The name comes from a grove of these blooming trees that previously existed here; they are no longer there. A French architect called Joseph Folléa constructed the Tuscan-style mansion and the formal gardens with oak trees that are there today. The area was once held by a well-to-do family of industrialists from Lyonnais; it was bought by the city in the 1970s and made available to the public as a green space.

Have fun with it: Explore the mountainous slopes of the La Croix Rousse district, formerly the hub of silk textile workers' workshops, and, today, one of the city's most intriguing, varied, and artistic neighborhoods, before seeing this gorgeous park and house. Have a picnic while admiring the manor's symmetrical architectural features and the natural surroundings. The Tuscan-inspired design is interestingly contrasted with painted murals and modern statuary.

6. Parc des Berges du Rhone

Av. Leclerc, Lyon, France 69007

This "green corridor" may be found next to the Musée des Confluences, a museum of modern art, along the banks of the Rhone river in the southern part of the city. A large grassy terrace area with views of the river and a north garden with groups of fig trees can be found in the park's upper region. A lush walkway, also bordered by poplar trees, can be seen in the lower area.

Having fun with it: In the morning, see a display at the Musée des Confluences before crossing the Pont Pasteur bridge to go to the riverfront park from the Presqu'Ile (Lyon's center "island" between the Rhone and Saône). Take a leisurely walk around the promenade and consider having a quick lunch on a seat. In addition, it's a terrific place to go biking and people-watch. Lastly, if you want to have a longer walk, go north along the Rhone to the city center or south till you reach the Parc de Gerland, another wonderful park, by taking the promenade.

CHAPTER 15: THE 10 MOST FAMOUS STRUCTURES AND LOCATIONS IN LYON

Travelers of all types will find Lyon to be a beautiful French city with a lot to offer, particularly if you're interested in viewing famous sites. You may visit many structures and sites from various times since the city itself is thousands of years old and was founded by the Romans.

You must have a plan for the sites and structures you wish to visit in Lyon if you want to make the most of your vacation there. Thankfully, a small number of them stand out from the crowd, so you may wish to give them priority. These are 10 of Lyon's most famous structures and locations.

1. Fourvière Basilica

The huge Fourvière Basilica is a non-Gothic church with an extraordinary architectural design that is dedicated to the Virgin Mary. Instead, it uses four major towers and a bell tower with a gilded figure of the Virgin Mary to combine Romanesque and Byzantine architectural styles.

You may experience its artistic splendor firsthand when you come, thanks to the exquisite stained glass and mosaics that decorate the inside. The structure is known as the "upside-down elephant" by the locals because the four towers resemble the creature's legs, and the building itself resembles its body. It is all located just across from Fourvière Station.

Address: 8 Pl. de Fourvière, Lyon, France, 69005

Open: Every day, 7 am to 6 pm

Phone: +33 (0)4 78 25 13 01

2. Bartholdi Fountain

The Bartholdi Fountain is a striking fountain made of lead that depicts a lady driving four mighty horses while seated in a chariot. The horses are supposed to symbolize France's most recognizable rivers, while the lady is meant to be a representation of France.

While the statue is essentially symmetrical, each feature is distinctive in its own way. It is a monument historique and made of lead, although having an iron frame to support it. The Plaza des Terreaux in Lyon's First Arr is where you may locate it.

Location: Place des Terreaux, Lyon, France, 69001

Open: 24/7

Phone: +33 (0)4 72 77 69 69

3. Place Bellecour

A large open plaza with two pavilions and elaborately carved sculptures, Place Bellecour, is located in the heart of Lyon. The Petit Prince and Antoine de Saint-Exupery are shown in the statue on the west end of the plaza, while King Louis XIV is portrayed in the monument in the center of the square riding a horse.

While you are exploring this sizable pedestrian plaza, it is recommended that you make use of the pavilions available to you. The first is aimed at giving information to tourists, while the second is an art gallery. It is entirely located in the town's center, at Carnot-Gailleton, between the Rhone and the Saone.

Location: Place, Lyon, France (69002)

Open: 24/7

Phone: +33 (0)4 72 77 69 69

4. Cathédrale Saint-Jean-Baptiste

The Cathédrale Saint-Jean-Baptiste, often known as the Lyon Cathedral, is a large Roman Catholic cathedral that is devoted to Saint John the Baptist. It took three centuries, from 1180 to 1480, to construct the church.

When you go, you may see its beautiful quality firsthand, but bear in mind that it still conducts routine operations that you shouldn't interrupt. Every December, it also holds the annual Festival of Light, which features illumination displays on the cathedral's front. This church may be found close to the riverbanks, southwest of Jardin Archéologique.

Location: Place Saint-Jean, Lyon, France, 69005

Open: Monday through Friday, 8.15 a.m. to 7.45 p.m., 8.15 a.m. to 7 p.m. on Saturday, and 8 a.m. to 7 p.m. on Sunday.

Phone: +33 (0)6 60 83 53 97

5. Teatro Galo-Romano

The town's Teatro Galo-Romano is an antique Roman amphitheater that is situated in the area where the old Roman city once stood. It was first built in 15 BCE when it had a diameter of just 90 meters, but the last phase of construction was finished at the beginning of the second century.

Although out of use by the third century, this theater is among the oldest and best maintained of its type. You will be in a UNESCO World Heritage Site while you are there. It is included in Fourviere Hill in the Fifth Arr.

Location: Rue de l'Antiquaille, Lyon, France 69005

Phone: +33 (0)4 72 38 49 30

6. Lyon Opera House

The National Opéra of Lyon is housed at the impressively designed Lyon Opera House (also known as Opera Nouvel). Its structure is distinctive since it has undergone several transformations throughout time. It was originally a rectangular Italian-style home with a horseshoe-shaped amphitheater when it was initially constructed in the 19th century.

You may see the improvements that the most recent architect, Nouvel, did when you visit this home now. It now has a steel and glass barrel vault on top, and the inner area has tripled in size thanks to below-ground excavation. It is located south of Place Louis Pradel on the east side of Pentes de la Croix Rousse.

Location: 1 Place de la Comédie, Lyon, France (6909).

Phone: +33 (0)4 69 85 54 54

7. Canuts Painted Wall

The Canuts Painted Wall is an enormous mural that displays a whole landscape with hyper-realistic images that reflect what everyday life is like in the La Croix-Rousse neighborhood. It's been a long since I've seen one of these, but I've been meaning to for a while.

You will be at one of the biggest public art exhibitions in all of Europe when you come. It is situated at the junction of Bd des Canuts and Rue Denfert-Rochereau, close to the heart of the La Croix - Rousse neighborhood.

Address: 36 Bd des Canuts, Lyon, France 69004

Open: 24/7

Phone: +33 (0)4 78 50 44 57

8. Tête d'Or Park

Tête d'Or Park, also known as the park of the golden head, is a 290-acre urban park with lush vegetation, trails, and a lake. You can even go boating on the lake if you come in the summer to get a new view of the park's stunning features.

There are many various things to do at this park, such as a velodrome, mini-golf, and mini-train. Even a little zoo is located there. Everything is located on the 6th Arr's north side.

Location: Lyon, France, 69006

Open: Everyday, 6:30 a.m. to 10:30 p.m.

Phone: +33 (0)4 72 69 47 60

9. Institute and Villa Lumière

The Institute and Villa Lumière is an organization and museum that is located in a lavish structure and is devoted to preserving significant facets of French cinema. It is located within the historic home of the Lumière family, who developed the cinematography, as the name indicates.

Even though the mansion is stunning in and of itself, you may tour some of the most significant filmmaking artifacts in the whole world when you are there. It is located on Monplaisir's northeastern side, only a short distance from the Monplaisir - Lumière Metro Station.

Place: 25 Rue du Premier Film, Lyon, France, 69008

Open: from Tuesday through Sunday, 10 a.m. to 6:30 p.m. (closed on Mondays)

Phone: +33 (0)4 78 78 18 95

10. Hôtel Dieu

The majestic hospital edifice known as Hôtel Dieu was constructed beside the river in the middle of the 15th century, although its origins are medieval. You'll discover a permanent display on the history of medical practice inside named Musee des Hospices Civils.

The structure itself, which extends out in both directions from that center spire, is ornamented with an attractive dome amid many windows. The location of the place being referred to is on the eastern side of Place Bellecour, situated next to the Rhône river.

Address: 1 Place de l'Hôpital, Lyon, France, 69002

Open: Everyday, 10 am to 8 pm

CHAPTER 16: HOW TO SPEND YOUR FIRST 48 HOURS IN LYON: THE ULTIMATE ITINERARY

Lyon is one of France's biggest and most interesting towns, nestled between the Burgundy wine region to the north and the French Mountains to the east. Lyon is both staunchly contemporary and has a long past, as seen by the stunning Roman remains, and Renaissance and medieval buildings found there. Its culinary scene is famous, and the city is a fascinating location to learn about modern French culture since it has many universities, museums, marketplaces, operas, and movies.

To see the finest of Lyon, follow this recommended two-day schedule. You may modify it as needed to suit your needs and interests.

Day 1: Morning

9 a.m.: After arriving at the Part-Dieu or Perrache railway stations or the Lyon International Airport, go directly to your hotel to drop off your baggage. To cut down on time spent driving from place to place, choose to lodge near or close to the city center.

The Presqu'île, Lyon's historic core, is your first destination. It is located on a strip of land that is situated between the Rhône and Saône River banks. Direct your attention to the magnificent Plaza des Terreaux, where you can see Lyon's Hôtel de Ville (City Hall) and the Bartholdi fountain, which was constructed in 1889 and has a striking equestrian sculpture.

Examine the treasures in the Musée des Beaux-Arts after admiring the area and its attractive café patios (Fine Arts Museum). The museum was erected on the old buildings of a 17th-century convent.

Next, leisurely make your way south to the large Place Bellecour by meandering through the busy retail lanes in the Cordeliers neighborhood. It is one of the biggest public squares in Europe and is well-known for its enormous Ferris wheel and an equestrian monument of King Louis XIV.

12:30 p.m.: Lunch is the perfect opportunity to experience Lyon's renowned culinary scene. Indulge in classic Lyonnais fare like pike dumplings (quenelles de brochet), fresh herbed cheese on bread (cervelle de canut), and pink praline pie for dessert at one of the Presqu'île's family-run bouchons. And consider sipping on some red or white wine from the region.

Day 1: Afternoon

2 p.m.: Following a leisurely lunch, cross the Saône River on the Passerelle Saint-Georges Bridge to see the Old Lyon (Old Lyon). See the Cathédrale Saint-Jean, a Roman and Gothic-style cathedral constructed between the 12th and 15th centuries, after taking in the views from the beautiful footbridge. The entrance is free.

Next, tour Rue Saint-many Jean's attractions, which include a museum of traditional puppetry and small boutiques and bakeries. As you meander around the region, take in the rose and ochre facades of Renaissance-era buildings and think about joining a guided tour to explore the complex courtyards and tunnels that link many of them. The French Resistance held covert meetings in several of them, which were locally known as traboules, during World War II. They were constructed in part to help merchants to convey products from the city's heights to its then-center.

Four o'clock: Ride one of the two funicular trains up Fourvière Hill after seeing Old Lyon (you can use a metro ticket or Lyon City Card if you have one). The primary remains of the Gallo-Roman city known as Lugdunum, which originally existed in what is now Lyon, are located on Fourvière Hill, one of Lyon's Unesco World Heritage Sites.

The Notre Dame de Fourvière Basilica, a significant Lyon monument from the late 19th century, is also located on Fouvrière Hill. Start here to take in the expansive panoramas of the whole city and its crimson roofs.

Afterward, go to the Gallo-Roman Museum around 5 o'clock. The museum, which was carved out of a hillside and had subterranean display areas, houses magnificent collections of ancient antiquities, including statues and sculptures, ceremonial items, jewelry, money, and other everyday items.

Even more spectacular are the two open-air Roman arenas. The biggest in France, the main amphitheater, formerly held up to 10,000 people, while the smaller theater (known as the Odéon) held around 3,000 people. The well-maintained arenas are still utilized to hold concerts and outdoor plays, particularly in the summer.

Day 1: Evening

6:30 p.m.: Return to Old Town by the Funicular or on foot, where you may then settle down for supper. One of the city's most well-known bouchons, Bouchon Les Lyonnais, is one to make reservations at if you're in the mood for something traditional. It is housed in a vaulted stone basement. Try Les Loges, a Michelin-starred restaurant with a table situated in a stunning courtyard from the fourteenth century, for a special event or romantic evening. The food here features inventive takes on classic Lyonnais fare.

9 p.m.: Following supper, meander through the dimly lighted streets of Vieux Lyon and the Presqu'île to view some of the city's famous structures, and monuments lit up at night. The Lyon Opera, the Hôtel de Ville, and the whole of Place des Terreaux, as well as the riverfront quays and bridges along the Saône and Rhône, are locations that are particularly picturesque at night. The architect Jean Nouvel created the futuristic, domed glass roof of the Lyon Opera.

10 p.m.: Stop by a pub on or near Plaza des Terreaux for a beverage or a glass of wine. We suggest L'Antiquaire, a speakeasy-style pub renowned for its distinctive drinks and hip atmosphere.

Day 2: Morning

8:30 a.m.: Start the day with breakfast on the Rhône River's right bank. For delicious coffee and tea, smoked fish, omelets, fresh pastries, fruit and juices, and other breakfast options, visit Le Kitchen Café.

Following that, stroll around the lively University neighborhood of the city, paying special attention to the areas of Place Jean-Macé and Rue de Chevreul. This is one of Lyon's less popular and more modern districts, where you may see scenes of ordinary students and local life while you browse the cafés, shops, and foreign food markets.

The Resistance and Deportation History Centre, which chronicles World War II events, Nazi persecution in the city, and the valor of Resistance leaders like Jean Moulin, is a good place to learn more about Lyon's darker past.

11:30 a.m.: Go west to the riverfront region and wander northward along the Berges du Rhône, a quayside promenade. You'll discover lovely boats and boat cafés, bike lanes, and leisure places as you explore this region, which is bordered by vegetation and grassy areas.

Day 2: Afternoon

12:30 p.m.: If your morning's worth of walking has left you hungry, you're in luck. The following visit, the Halles de Lyon Paul-Bocuse market, provides lots of opportunities for trying some of the city's greatest gastronomic products. You can either sit down at one of the informal eateries in or near the market for a quick lunch or pick up something to go with you. No matter what you choose, be sure to carve out some time to browse the market's hundreds of booths, which offer everything from fresh fruit and vegetables to wines and chocolates. Moreover, this is a great spot to acquire presents or nonperishable foods to carry back on the aircraft.

2:30 p.m.: Next, go to the Park de la Tête d'Or, Lyon's biggest park, by taking Rue Garibaldi north for approximately 15 minutes. With hundreds of trees and plants, artificial lakes, strolling routes, lush lawns, and play areas, the romantic-style park is a verdant paradise. If you opt to bring products from the market to enjoy outside, settle down for a picnic.

4:30 p.m.: Leave the park and walk south until you reach the Croix-Paquet metro station. Cross the Rhône River at the Bridge de Lattre-de-Tassigny. Take Metro line C to the Hénon station by boarding. You've reached the Croix-Rousse neighborhood at this point. It was formerly the center of Lyon's textile and silk trading sector, but now it is a hip, bohemian neighborhood with a very rural feel.

Begin at the "Mur des Canuts," a large mural painted on a building's façade. As a trompe l'oeil (visual illusion), it shows steep steps and images from the neighborhood's everyday and historical life.

Afterward, go around the nearby streets and Place de la Croix-Rousse, the city's principal plaza. Pre-dinner drinks may be had on a patio at your preferred bar.

Day 2: Evening

6:30 p.m.: As the sun starts to set (or as dusk settles on the horizon, depending on the time of year), head to the Place Colbert, an elevated square with benches, to see a wide view of the city. One of Lyon's most remarkable traboules, the Cour des Voraces, is located at #9. It has a dizzying exterior stairway that rises six floors high. This structure and several others in the neighborhood serve as reminders of the city's past as a center for silk workers (canuts) and their activities.

7:30 p.m.: It's time for supper, and the thriving Croix-Rousse neighborhood offers a wide variety of choices. We advise making a reservation at a hip restaurant like Bistrot des Voraces, a wine bar where you can choose from a large selection of wines to go with seasonal small plates and entrees. The classic Lyonnais bouchon is modernized at Daniel et Denise, which is regarded as one of the greatest restaurants in the area.

Have you got more energy? There are several places to have a nightcap in the neighborhood, including pubs and clubs. Le Chantecler is a go-to destination for summertime beverages out on the spacious terrace, while The Monkey Club is a well-known cocktail bar staffed by expert mixologists.

CHAPTER 17: TEN MISTAKES TOURISTS MAKE IN LYON

Avoid These Mistakes on Your First Trip to Lyon

There are relatively few severe errors that individuals make while they are in Lyon. They won't likely result in anything more than a small amount of shame and a small financial waste. In general, Lyon is a highly secure and welcoming city for tourists. Thus difficulties are uncommon.

Yet there will always be harmless mistakes you may make since you don't know any better when you go to a new place. To assist you in avoiding them, we have chosen the most prevalent ones you should be aware of. So don't worry; even the worst can be avoided with just a little common sense and basic personal safety.

1. Failure to get a Lyon City Card

You'll be losing out on substantial savings.

The Lyon City Card is a well-liked method for making your trip to Lyon as convenient and reasonably priced as possible. Use of the metro, trams, buses, and funicular trains are all included in the price of the card, and entrance to 23 different museums is free as well.

You may purchase passes good for one to four days. Longer stays inevitably increase the cost, but they also become much more cost-effective since you have more opportunities to take advantage of the advantages they provide. You may purchase cards online and arrange to pick them up in Lyon or have them delivered to you. Tickets are good for 18 months, so you may even postpone your vacation without squandering your money.

2. Visiting the traboules at peak time

They are both little and well-liked.

The traboules, a network of secret passages that run throughout Lyon's historic center, set the city apart from other French cities. They were first built to make it fast and simple for residents to travel between their dwellings and the city's major water sources. Later, merchants used them to transport more costly goods, notably silks, in a secure manner. Even during World War Two, they are credited for facilitating the covert movements of the French Resistance.

Just roughly 40 of the original hundreds of traboules are still accessible to the general public. Although being seen as "hidden," they are really quite well-liked by travelers. In fact, the amount of individuals utilizing the little places has become a major source of dissatisfaction for the locals. It is advisable to explore these distinctive thoroughfares in the late afternoon after the scheduled excursions have ended. Furthermore, make an effort to be silent and polite.

3. Intentionally driving around the city

The environment is not conducive to cars.

The majority of travel recommendations for persons who want to drive around France strongly advise against visiting Lyon due to the city's horrendous traffic. This city is among the largest and oldest in the country, and its streets are mainly characterized by winding and narrow roads that are not well-suited for heavy vehicular traffic.

Thankfully, there isn't really any justification for even thinking about hiring a vehicle in Lyon. The majority of the major attractions are concentrated around the pedestrian-friendly city center, and there is a good and comprehensive public transportation system. There's even a really excellent bike-share system in action. You would be better off acquiring a decent map of the metro system and understanding which stations are close to what attractions than investing time and money in purchasing a vehicle.

4. Purchasing fake Metro cards

There are several language choices at the vending machines.

The ticketing system is often the most perplexing and unsettling aspect of utilizing public transportation. Do you own the correct ticket? Does it have the greatest pricing for the journey, and will it get you where you want to go? When you're not acquainted with the network, it's difficult to tell. Some kind people may offer to sell you a ticket straight in order to expedite the procedure. Sadly, these people are con artists.

Ticket touts often approach travelers who seem to be lost and try to sell them false or expired tickets. This is especially widespread at the Part-Dieu station since it is the closest to the main railway station. If somebody does so, disregard them. The personnel at the metro is really helpful and polite. Because there are several language alternatives for the instructions, even the vending machines aren't too challenging to understand.

5. Underestimating the potential heat of the summer months

Also, failure to properly box

Very likely, you don't picture Lyon having a tropical climate in your mind. But from June through August, it becomes a little bit hotter here than it does in Nice. In actuality, they are comparable to the coastal temperatures of Morocco.

The same kinds of risks are present at high temperatures, just as they are in tropical climes. In addition to packing or purchasing sunscreen, remember to stay hydrated and even plan for mosquitoes in the nighttime.

6. Giving money to fake charity workers

Or letting them divert your attention

In several major towns in France as well as other renowned tourist locations around Europe, charity workers are extremely prevalent. Unfortunately, not everyone is attempting to improve the world; others just care about their own interests. Where there are charity workers, there will always be charity fraudsters as well. These are especially prevalent in Lyon around Rue de la République, Part-Dieu station, and Gare du Lyon.

A true charity worker would never approach you on the street and beg for money. This is a fairly easy technique to distinguish between the real ones and the fakes. Your email address is the only information they'll need to send you a newsletter. Keep in mind that if you stop for a discussion in any well-known tourist location, the bogus charity scammer may be a pickpocket's diversion, so keep a check on your belongings.

7. Eating at a scammy restaurant

By failing to carefully consider what you are purchasing

The finest location in the world to eat is undoubtedly Lyon, which is recognized as France's gastronomic capital. The vast majority of eateries live up to that reputation, offering top-notch food at reasonable prices. A few businesses, nevertheless, capitalize on this reputation and use it as cover to attempt to con their clients.

Fortunately, it's not too difficult to identify the strategies they use. If you don't clarify that you just want a small or medium dish, you could discover that a huge one arrives. Perhaps you can simply discover products on your bill that you didn't order. Tourist-only menus (with higher costs) and important information about the meal hidden in the fine print—inevitably printed only in French—are a little difficult to detect. Stick to well-regarded restaurants (including those we suggest) or thoroughly review your menu and your bill to prevent overpaying.

8. Forgetting to make a reservation for that special supper

You could pass on a delicious supper.

Lyon draws gastronomes by the planeload because of its stellar reputation for top-notch cuisine, particularly during the busy seasons. Although the city has a huge selection of restaurants, there is a very significant probability that the top ones will be completely booked most nights well in advance of opening time, sometimes even days in advance.

We highly suggest making reservations in advance if you're planning a special supper at one of Lyon's top eateries, including the ones we highlight in our guide to the city. It's better to make reservations at least a few days in advance if you plan to eat out on the weekend. Although weekdays are often less hectic, it is still preferable to avoid hunger.

9. Remaining on Rue Ste Catherine till it closes

Or, really, any location with a vibrant nightlife.

It practically goes without saying that inebriated individuals sometimes make poor decisions and occasionally even do harmful things. Wherever in the globe where alcohol is available freely, this is true. This is particularly true in Lyon, where the Rue Saint Catherine neighborhood is the center of the city's nightlife.

In these places, the police are often more visible, particularly around 3 am when the pubs shut. They can't be everywhere at once, however, so some danger is unavoidable. The best course of action is to be aware of these hazards and take any necessary precautions.

10. Choose a location for your lodging outside of the city center.

It's a waste of money.

The majority of the lodging choices and the majority of Lyon's greatest attractions are situated in and around the city center. In light of this, you may be tempted to reserve a vacation rental or cheap hotel in a remote area. You should be aware, however, that your time and money won't be well spent on this. The outer arrondissements are not as properly policed as the inner ones, so in addition to spending a significant amount of time each day traveling back into the city center, you won't be able to enjoy it as much. Sometimes it might be hazardous to explore these regions, particularly at night.

Choose Part-Dieu on the Rhône's eastern bank if you're searching for a place that offers some economy without compromising comfort and safety. Instead, for additional choices on where to stay in Lyon, have a look at our neighborhood guide.

CONCLUSION

Practical Advice From Lyon On Traveling, Being Safe, And More

The charming and ancient city of Lyon is situated in France's Rhône-Alpes region. It is renowned for its beautiful architecture, extensive history, and superb cuisine. The city has a sizable local population in addition to being a well-liked tourist attraction. In this guide, we will give practical advice about getting around, keeping safe, and more in Lyon.

Getting Around:

Lyon offers a first-rate public transportation system that consists of buses, trams, and a metro. In an an an an a. .... All metro stations and the majority of tram stops have ticket machines where you may purchase tickets. Bus drivers may also sell you tickets, although they only take coins. The price of a single ticket is 1.90 euros and its hourly validity.

A, B, C, and D are the four lines that makeup Lyon's metro system. The lines are color-coded, and each line has its unique path. The metro is a quick and effective means to get through the city. Depending on the line, the metro operates from roughly 5:00 am until midnight.

Six lines, denoted by the letters T1, T2, T3, T4, T5, and T6, make up Lyon's tram network. Each tram line has its own route, and the trams are likewise color-coded. Depending on the line, the trams operate from around 4:30 in the morning until midnight.

Almost 130 routes make up Lyon's extensive bus network, which traverses the whole city. The buses are an excellent method to get about, particularly if you're going somewhere where the metro or tram doesn't go.

Vélo'v, a bike-sharing program, is available in Lyon in addition to public transit. With more than 350 stations located all around the city, there are more than 4,000 bikes accessible. A credit card or a Vélo'v card, which you may get online or at any Vélo'v station, can be used to hire a bike.

Staying Safe:

Lyon is a safe city, but like any large city, there are some safety concerns. The following advice can help you remain safe while visiting Lyon:

1. Be aware of your surroundings: Be alert of any unusual activities and pay attention to your surroundings. If you have a question, please feel free to contact us.

2. Store your valuables in a secure location. This includes your passport, wallet, and phone. In public areas, do not leave them unattended.

3. Avoid wandering alone in secluded or dark areas: This is particularly important at night.

4. Call a trustworthy taxi company or utilize an official taxi stand if you need to take a cab. Never board a taxi driven by an unauthorized person.

5. Monitor your beverages: Be careful with your drinks while visiting pubs or clubs, and never take drinks from total strangers.

6. Be cautious while using ATMs: Keep an eye on your surroundings and avoid becoming distracted when using an ATM. Safeguard your PIN number.

7. Obey traffic regulations: Whether you're bicycling or driving, obey traffic regulations and pay attention to pedestrians.

8. Have emergency contact information on hand: In case of an emergency, keep contact information on hand for the police and ambulance.

Things to See and Do:

Lyon offers a wide variety of sights and activities. The following are a few of Lyon's main attractions:

1. Basilique Notre-Dame de Fourvière: Perched atop Fourvière Hill, this magnificent church gives wonderful views of the city. The basilica is a must-see site in Lyon and a superb example of 19th-century architecture.

2. Vieux Lyon: Also known as Old Lyon, this charming historic area is home to magnificent cathedrals, Renaissance-style buildings, and winding cobblestone lanes. Several of Lyon's top eateries and coffee shops may be found there as well.

3. Musée des Beaux-Arts de Lyon: This magnificent museum is home to a sizable collection of artwork, including pieces by well-known creators like Monet, Picasso, and Van Gogh.

4. Park de la Tête d'Or: The biggest urban park in France, this lovely park provides a tranquil haven from the bustle of the city. It has various walking and cycling lanes, a lake, a rose garden, and a zoo.

5. Croix-Rousse: This vibrant area is well-known for its past involvement in the silk industry. It has a bohemian atmosphere and is home to many artists. On top of a hill, it gives breathtaking views of the city.

6. Les Halles de Lyon-Paul Bocuse: For foodies, this indoor market is a culinary haven. There are around 60 merchants there, offering anything from baked products and fresh fish to cheese and charcuterie.

7. Musée Miniature et Cinéma: This one-of-a-kind museum displays small replicas of iconic movie sets and props, as well as special effects and animatronics.

8. Opéra de Lyon: Opera, ballet, and other performances are presented at this lovely 19th-century theater. It is a fantastic location to explore Lyon's vibrant cultural scene.

Food and Drink:

Lyon is well-known for its superb cuisine, and there are numerous foods and beverages that you just must taste while there. Some of the best Lyon specialties are listed below:

1. Coq au Vin: Chicken is cooked in red wine and served with mushrooms, onions, and bacon in this traditional French meal. It is a filling and delicious supper.

2. Quenelles: A combination of fish or meat and breadcrumbs is used to make these oval-shaped dumplings. They are often given to you with a creamy sauce.

3. Salade Lyonnaise: This dish consists of frisée lettuce, bacon, croutons, and an egg that has been poached, all of which are combined with a warm vinaigrette.

4. Bouchons: Lyon is famous for its bouchons, which are quaint, traditional eateries that provide substantial, down-home fare. They are an excellent way to see Lyon's culinary scene since they often serve regional delicacies.

5. Cervelle de Canut: Fresh cheese, herbs, and spices are used to make this cheese spread. Crudités or bread are frequently served with it.

6. Beaujolais Wine: Lyon is situated in the Beaujolais wine area, and while in the city, you should definitely sample some of the local wine.

7. Café Comptoir Abel: Since 1933, this renowned Lyon café has served coffee and pastries. It's a fantastic location to enjoy Lyon's café scene.

Conclusion

Lyon is a beautiful and energetic city with a fascinating history, top-notch cuisine, and a thriving arts and cultural scene. In addition to having a big local population, it is a well-liked tourist attraction. Lyon offers a first-rate public transit infrastructure that makes getting about the city simple. Lyon is a safe city, but it's still a good idea to pay attention to your surroundings and exercise care. From ancient ruins to contemporary museums and galleries, Lyon has a lot to see and do. And no visit to Lyon would be complete without sampling some of the mouthwatering local cuisine and beverages.

Made in the USA
Coppell, TX
05 January 2024